Railways: Mechanical Engineering

J. B. Snell was born in Suva, Fiji, in 1932, and the first railways he saw were the local narrow-gauge sugar-cane systems which, like much older lines, used both steam and animal power. Railways therefore have been in his blood since an early age. Following an education at Bryanston and Oxford, he devoted some years to a career in public transport administration, first with London Transport and later with British Railways. However, in 1968 he reluctantly accepted the shrinking horizons in this branch of the public service, resigned, and is now starting again in the wholly different field of the Law, while retaining an active interest in the preservation of some older and odder railways.

His first book, *Jennie*, a work of juvenile fiction, was published in 1958. Since then he has written several books on railway history and development, including *Britain's Railways under Steam* (1965).

Other titles in this Industrial Archaeology series published by Arrow Books

Railways: Civil Engineering by Bryan Morgan
Navigable Waterways by L. T. C. Rolt
Roads and Vehicles by Anthony Bird

J. B. Snell

Railways: Mechanical Engineering

ARROW BOOKS

ARROW BOOKS LTD
3 Fitzroy Square, London W1

AN IMPRINT OF THE HUTCHINSON GROUP

London Melbourne Sydney Auckland
Wellington Johannesburg Cape Town
and agencies throughout the world

*

First published by
The Longman Group Ltd 1971
Arrow edition 1973

This book is published at a net price and supplied subject to the Publishers Association Standard Condition of Sale registered under the Restrictive Trade Practices Act 1956

Made and printed in Great Britain
by C. Nicholls & Company Ltd
The Philips Park Press, Manchester M11 4AU

ISBN 0 09 908170 9

Contents

List of Illustrations

Line Drawings in the Text

Introduction

'Archaeology', in general, means the study of the past through its relics; the gaining of an understanding of a past way of life through an imaginative reconstruction based on surviving artefacts. The ordinary consequence of this is that the time studied is, at the very least, some centuries and often some thousands of years gone by. Closer times are better documented and there is seldom any need to go and dig to discover facts about them: they are on file in libraries.

Industrial Archaeology is thus a bit of an anomaly. It does not relate to the distant past, or only to a limited extent; for it studies nothing more ancient than the recently finished paragraphs of the chapter of history that is still being written. Arguably, industrialization is the most important material thing to have happened to mankind since our woolly ancestors discovered fire or the plough; but it has only just happened.

Even apart from its newness, any study of the industrial past differs from classical archaeology in another important way, precisely because it is indeed better documented. Not, by any means, all of it; the record is patchy, and here and there are departments of activity pursued by men following a day-to-day bread-and-butter grind, pioneering but with no thought of making history or records. But in general the technology has been quite well written up and contemporary accounts can be found if one knows where to look for them. And fortunately for the historian, the nineteenth century was not the equal of the twentieth in the sheer appalling bulk of published matter on scientific and technical matters; the man who one day comes to write the industrial history of our own times will have quite a different sort of problem.

Better records bring another difference. In ancient times nearly all men are shadows to us, and even when their names and their deeds have come down we are still usually left wondering what they looked like, what their motives were, and a host of unresolved little details of circumstance that could be resolved with more accounts by descriptive eye-witnesses. But we know enough about a Stephenson or a Brunel to feel we can understand them, and the scenes they saw can spring authentically to life through accounts their contemporaries have left. What it was like to walk through the gardens of Babylon must be largely conjecture; what it was like to stand on the footplate of the *Rocket* as she hurtled along faster than any man had moved before we know, for we have been told.

This book is one of two companion volumes which set out to give an account of the early part of the Railway Age in Britain. In the other book, Bryan Morgan has given a history of railway civil engineering during the period of construction: the present volume attempts an account of railway mechanical engineering, up to about 1860. The division between the two fields is sometimes a little arbitrary, but in general the rule has been 'if it moves, it's mechanical'. But the nature of this division has imposed the need for a different approach in each case. Most of the civil artefacts of the railway age are still with us, and in use: indeed, very many of them will remain to puzzle our descendants in two thousand years' time. Bryan Morgan has therefore had a field of study much more 'archaeological' than the present author's. For most of the artefacts of the mechanical side have disappeared, though an impressive number, all things considered, still remain; the *Rocket* and the *Sans Pareil* still confront each other at South Kensington. But the undiscriminating pressure of day-to-day affairs, and the fact that railway machinery is large and expensive, have removed from the scene all concrete traces of some of the most formative developments. Hence, on this side of the boundary, there has to be more reliance on the written record. The subject is a vast one, and this book is no more than a superficial guide or index to it. But even this seems worth attempting.

Sometimes one hears people ask why the study of transport systems should be considered a subject deserving of much interest; they feel surprise that it should attract attention which might otherwise be devoted to some of the higher achievements of human endeavour, to philosophy, religion, war and statecraft, music, literature, painting, sculpture. The answer seems a simple one. A human community is alive only through the communication which exists between the men who compose it. Communication, once you are out of sight or earshot, involves transport. A human body is alive only because its heart beats and circulates blood through it, communicating with every cell and extremity. The two organisms are similar. One marvels at the dreaming spires readily enough; but their foundations are just as deserving of study. Michelangelo did not consider the task of hauling the marble for his statues down from the mountain quarries of Carrara too menial for him.

'God bless the man wi' peace and plenty
That first invented metal plates!
Draw out his years till five times twenty
Then slide him through the heavenly gates.'

T. WILSON (1799)
on Iron Rails

CHAPTER ONE

Railways Before Mechanical Power

If one discounts the use of rutways in classical times, the first ancestors of the railway appeared in mines. Mining for coal and ores had continued even through the Dark Ages; it was, however, a branch of human activity that had little attraction for the literate minority, and so it went for many centuries largely unrecorded. Georg Bauer, 'Agricola' (1494–1555), was an exception; his life's work, published in 1556, was the great book *De Re Metallica*, which describes in great detail, with many illustrations, mining principles and practice in Hungary, Bohemia, Saxony, and the Harz Mountains, bringing a vivid picture to life. The book is not only the best account we have of medieval mining; for two centuries it was the standard textbook for mining engineers. (In 1912 a modern edition, edited and translated by Herbert Hoover, later President of the USA, was produced; this in turn was a work of reference consulted, among others, by Walt Disney, whose Seven Dwarfs wore the costumes of Agricola's miners, even if Snow White did not.) Even in the sixteenth century, the shafts of some mines in Austria were already over a thousand feet deep, and a considerable technology of pumping and ventilation, not to mention hoists and lifts, powered by horse-gins and waterwheels, had been developed. The advantage of some kind of prepared trackway, which could smooth the way for loaded wagons over rough surfaces and guide them through dark, narrow passages underground, was sufficiently obvious for men capable of mastering these more difficult problems to have no trouble in finding a solution; though as it happens the only clear drawing of such a wagon in Agricola shows that it ran on a trackway of planks, with plain wheels on a flat surface, and was guided by a pin following a groove.

It is not at all clear where the idea of a flanged wheel running on a rail was first put into practice, since details for the next two centuries are scanty. But Germany's claim to have first carried out this particular development is rather weakened by the fact that by the time horse tramways were in wide use in the Ruhr district, towards the end of the eighteenth century, they were known as 'Englischer Kohlenweg'. Gray's *Chorographia*, an account of the lands and trades of Newcastle upon Tyne and Northumberland, published in 1649, mentions that one Master Beaumont, who commenced mining in Nottinghamshire in 1602 and around Newcastle in 1608, introduced 'many rare engines, not known in these parts; As . . . Waggons with one horse to carry down Coales from the Pits'. Lord Keeper Guildford, a judge of the Northern Circuit in 1676, had cause in a written judgment to describe the wagons and wagonways then existing around Newcastle as follows. 'The manner of the carriage [of coal] is by laying rails of timber from the colliery down to the river, exactly straight and parallel; and bulky carts are made with four rowlets, fitting these rails, whereby the carriage is so easy, that one horse will draw down 4 or 5 chaldrons of coals' (or about 2¼ tons, compared with the load of ¾–1 ton that might be drawn on an ordinary road).

By the middle of the eighteenth century, railways had gone through three main stages of evolution since the primitive mine-tub illustrated by Agricola. They had emerged from the depths of mines and the recesses of quarries and factories; they had begun to discard wooden rails for iron; and they had, equally tentatively, begun to change from wooden wheels to iron ones. The development of permanent way, and the pattern of the change to iron during that development, is dealt with by Bryan Morgan in the companion volume. It is sufficient to note here that although the first iron rails appear to have been laid at Coalbrookdale by Reynolds in November 1767, demonstrating at once what saving in tractive effort they made possible, these were no more than cast iron faceplates laid on top of the old wooden rails. The first successful self-supporting iron rails were probably used in South Wales about 1791, after a series of experiments in other parts of the country.

Iron wheels came rather earlier, about 1754. According to Nicholas Wood, they were first used on the incline railway at Bath. Simple castings, they were easy to make and they lasted long; that they wore rather harshly on wooden rails mattered less, since simple squared-off timbers were cheap enough and quick to replace, especially as generally the wooden rails were in two parts, and only an easily removed top section took the wear. Wooden wheels were something of a problem; they were more expensive to make, and they had a relatively short life. They had to be used, though, for one reason: braking. Most of the mining districts were far from level, and even though some lines had considerable works of civil engineering to ease gradients, there were a lot of steep runs, as fierce sometimes as 1 in 20. Wooden wheels held the brake rather better on these. So for a long time it was normal for wagons to have a pair of iron wheels at one end, but wooden ones at the other, borne on by a simple brakeshoe attached to a lever on which the driver could sit when necessary to apply the brake. Going down a run the horse would be taken out of the traces and allowed to trail behind, putting the cart before the horse in a way that was considered one of the remarkable sights of the district; but at least this meant that if the brake failed, the horse would not be killed or injured through being run down.

Accidents were frequent. Steel and iron rails when wet get slippery enough, but wooden ones were far worse. Wagons 'running amain' were a common sight, and although men or boys were employed to scatter sand and ashes on the rails on the steeper declivities, it was often a case of rain stopping play. Many of the lines were unusable for this reason in wet weather, and traffic had to cease, while a sudden shower of rain might cause a mass breakaway and send every wagon on some miles of track slithering uncontrollably down to a fearful pile of destruction at the bottom of the hill. Sometimes men stood ready to hold a rope or chain across the line to hold a runaway, but this could not do much to stop a flyer whose driver had already jumped to save his skin.

The single-wheel brake was of course adequate in dry weather. But the simple lever which worked it meant that one driver could not be in charge of more than one wagon. In 1764 an arrangement of linked levers known as the 'long brake' was described by which one man sitting on the brake in the normal way at the back of one wagon could also actuate the brake of a second, but this device was not much used and perhaps only suited the moderate grades of certain particular lines; in general each pit had its own independent railway to the river or the sea, and although it might cross another, junctions or shared facilities and equipment were uncommon. It was not until about 1790, it seems, that the familiar cranked lever system we now know, applying brakes to all four wheels, was invented; and this was about the time when the use of iron for all wheels and rails began to be accepted.

The earliest British wagonways certainly used flanged wheels. This system had the advantage that the track was simpler, while the putting of a guiding flange on one edge of a wheel was a matter of no great difficulty, even when using wood. There was of course the drawback that such a wheel could not then be used on ordinary roads, while normal flangeless road wheels could not pass along the wagonway; but this was not a very serious matter. The business of the wagonway was entirely self-contained, and it was simple enough to lay tracks anywhere the wagons had cause to go. The flanged wheel/squared rail system is universal today, so the word 'railway' is now synonymous with it, covering both genus and species. But during the time that there *was* another species of railway, it was distinguished from that other by being called the 'edge railway'.

The opposite system, in which a plain flat wheel runs along the level foot of an L-shaped rail, developed much later. John Smeaton perhaps originated it, around 1756, but the earliest record of it is by John Curr, whose *Coal Viewer's and Engine Builder's Practical Companion* (1797) has some plates giving considerable detail of railways working on this principle, although these are in fact two-foot gauge affairs intended for underground use. Curr appears to have been responsible for an outdoor line of this type some ten years earlier, and possibly another railway two miles long that he built near Sheffield in 1775 (destroyed almost at once by an angry mob which forced him to hide in fear of his life for three days in the woods) was on the same principle. To distinguish them from edge railways, lines of this type are generally called 'plateways'.

Plateways were fairly uncommon outside South Wales, but there they were the most popular system. For a time they were technically ahead of the edge railway, partly because the details of pointwork, etc., were better thought out and because able engineers like Jessop, Outram, and Overton promoted them energetically, and partly because the first successful use of iron for rails complete in themselves happened to be achieved by plateway partisans. The necessity to cast a vertical lip or flange on the tramplate gave it the vertical or load-bearing strength which earlier iron rails had lacked; the kinship of rails with girders was not then fully appreciated, since attention had been directed to the use of iron simply as a means of reducing rolling resistance. But once the penny had dropped, and edge rails began to be made with a vertical component placed centrally under the loadbearing surface, the plateway's superiority was at an end. Such a rail was structurally stronger, weight for weight, than a tramplate, where the vertical component had inevitably to be on one side.

The plateway's protagonists had claimed that it gave less friction than the edge railway; this might have been so at first, when the competition was between iron and wood, but now it was the opposite of truth. For dirt and gravel, flung up by horses' hooves or in other ways, could lodge in the tramplate, where it was difficult to remove and so greatly increased frictional resistance. On the edge rail, dirt simply tended to fall off. The plateway's other claimed advantage, that it allowed the use of vehicles which could also pass on ordinary roads, was not in practice very valuable, as we have seen, and also it was found that there were considerable practical difficulties about designing front axles that were steerable on roads and capable of being locked solid on rails. One plateway in the Forest of Dean, worked by horses, survived until the mid-1930s; but the big conversion to edge railways in South Wales took place around 1849. C. F. Dendy Marshall, in his *British Railways Down to the Year 1830*, quotes Overton as saying both that plateways had less friction, and also that they were more practical on steep gradients, as a horse could hold back a bigger load while going downhill. He must have been a born salesman.

The nature of friction was at this time very little understood. As late as 1838 Nicholas Wood could still write: 'There is no subject in science, perhaps, on which there is a greater diversity of opinion, than in the laws which govern friction.' Alexander Gordon, a road-building civil engineer of some standing in his profession, could in 1837 calmly point out the distinction between the friction between wheel and rail, and that between axle and bearing, which was just beginning to be publicly appreciated (Nicholas Wood called them 'Friction of Rolling' and 'Friction of Attrition' respectively), and then proceeded to condemn railways out of hand as bubbles and frauds, since their wheels, like road wheels, had axles and bearings with similar frictional resistances. He saw little merit in railways compared with good roads, for this one reason. By this time he was swimming against the tide; but twenty years earlier it was a different matter, and the whole field was almost unexplored. There was considerable difficulty in devising experiments to test the two types of friction separately, but it was simple enough to arrive at values for friction per ton weight (including both 'rolling' and 'attrition') on rail, and then similar values for road by using the same vehicle.

Nicholas Wood conducted numerous experiments on frictional resistance on the Killingworth and Hetton railways in 1818–19, which are described in the first (1825) edition of his *Practical Treatise on Railroads;* some of these were made jointly with his colleague George Stephenson. He built a dynamometer car, consisting of a heavy pendulum mounted in a wagon, measuring the drawbar pull of a gang of men against a scale. One of the first practical results Wood came to was to realize the vast importance of proper lubrication, which was quite enough to explain the considerable experimental variations that he and others had found. Wood settled on neatsfoot oil for his experiments, but this was rather too expensive for general use. George Rennie conducted a series of experiments with lubricants around the same time, comparing tallow, vegetable oils, hogslard, soft soap, and his own private 'anti-attrition mixture'. Tallow was most generally used. The subject remained one of very vexed interest until well into the locomotive era.

Most of Wood's experiments consisted in settling wagons rolling down long inclines, and timing and measuring their run. This is quite a powerful method of investigation, and he even succeeded in obtaining a value for the internal resistance of one of Stephenson's early locomotives, which was too stiff to roll downhill on its own, by including it in a train of wagons of known resistance and setting it off, steamless, in company with them. In this way Wood was able to construct tables showing both the weights that could be hauled by a given power on the level, and also the effect of gradients, which were basic data for engineers contemplating any serious railwaybuilding activities. However, they did need later amplification. It was through too great a reliance on Wood's work that Dionysius Lardner made his famous miscalculation, in evidence before a Parliamentary Committee in 1834, as to the appalling speeds that would be reached if a train broke away on the 1 in 100 through Box Tunnel. Excusing himself in 1842, Lardner wrote that his evidence 'overlooked the influences brought into play by the rapidity of motion, and erred in forming too early generalizations from data still imperfect, applying the same standard to weigh the opposing forces whether the train were proceeding at the speed of a steamboat on the ocean, or winging its way through air with the swiftness of an eagle's flight'.

The other half of Wood's work consisted in measuring haulage power, and the effect that a given effort would obtain on rail, on road, and on canal. He found that a very large and powerful horse could exert a pull of 174 lb on starting, and of 125 lb while moving at 2½ mph, while an average horse could record figures about 20 per cent less. Either could keep the 2½ mph effort up practically for twenty miles a day continuously, with one rest day in every four or five. But at higher speeds most of the horse's effort went into moving itself, until its effective pull fell to nothing at all at about 12 mph.

Some of the practical consequences of this make interesting reading now. On ordinary road and canal work, where speeds were round two or three miles an hour, and on railway work where they were considerably faster but correspondingly less strenuous, a horse could work constantly over a full life, achieving an average of some twenty miles a day. The load hauled by a single horse on a railway was about 12 tons. On scheduled passenger coaches in the Liverpool area in the early 1820s, Wood found that 2304 coach-miles were operated daily, one 2-ton coach and four horses, at an average speed of 10 mph; but 709 horses were employed for the work, each covering on average thirteen miles a day but producing only 5¼ ton-miles a day compared with 192 on the railway. Further, after three years' work the coach-horse was fit only for the knackers.

The ability of a railway to multiply a horse's haulage capacity was a matter of great public wonderment whenever a new line was built in a new area. A newspaper account of a wager in 1805 is given, laid by a Mr Banks on the opening of the tramroad from Croydon to Merstham, an extension of the Surrey Iron Railway. Banks bet 'that a common horse could draw 36 tons for 6 miles, from a dead start'.

> Twelve wagons loaded with stone, each weighing over 3 tons, were chained together, and a horse taken promiscuously from the timber cart of Mr Harwood was yoked into the team. He started from the 'Fox' public-house, and drew the immense chain of

> wagons with apparent ease to near the turnpike at Croydon, a distance of 6 miles, in 1 hour 49 minutes. In the course of this time he stopped four times, to show that it was not by the impetus of the descent that the power was acquired, and after each stoppage drew off the chain of wagons from a dead rest. Having gained his wager, Mr Banks directed four more loaded wagons to be added to the cavalcade, with which the same horse again set off. And still further to show the effect of the railway in facilitating motion, he directed the attending workmen, to the number of about 50, to mount into the wagons, and the horse proceeded, without the least distress.

After the trial, the train was weighed, and the sixteen wagons plus the workmen were found to total 55¼ tons. All in all, it was a splendid piece of public relations for the Croydon, Merstham and Godstone.

Horses were not the only means of propulsion, even before steam; there was also the force of gravity. This was used in two ways; more rarely on a railway laid out on a continuous gradual fall, so that trains could roll unaided downhill in one direction, perhaps with the horse riding at its ease in a 'dandy-cart', but having to earn its corn pulling the load back hard uphill in the other direction. The most famous such railway in Britain is now the Festiniog, which was built quite late for a line of this kind (1836), but there were a number of others, complete with dandy-cars, in the coalfields. The commoner use of gravity as a power source was on the self-acting incline, a relatively short and sharp gradient connecting two different levels, on the analogy of a flight of locks on a canal, in which descending loaded wagons, by means of a cable and a windinghouse at the summit, drew up as a partial counterbalance empty wagons proceeding in the opposite direction. Since mines and quarries often tend to be on high ground, this was a very practical and convenient means of conveyance. Some self-acting inclines still exist here and there, in Northumberland, North Wales, and elsewhere, but they are now rapidly disappearing. It seems that the first one was again due to Reynolds of Coalbrookdale, who installed an incline (to carry canal boats, avoiding the need for locks and their water supply) in the Ketley ironworks in 1788.

Generally such inclines were fairly simple in operation; there would normally be a considerable excess of power which would have to be controlled by a strong brake working on the cable drum in the windinghouse. But an interesting account of both kinds of gravity working on two lines at Whitehaven, including a most unusual and ingenious self-acting incline, is given by Richard Ayton in his *Voyage round Great Britain* (1813).

Some of the pits lie at a considerable distance from the town, and the coals are conveyed from them to the vessels in wagons containing 45 cwt. each, and running upon rail-roads. It would appear no easy matter on a first sight to conduct these heavy loads with safety down the steep faces of the hills which flank the town, but it is managed without any kind of difficulty or danger. The wagons descend down the east hill by a road cut in traverses, each under the direction of one man, who mounts up behind, and pressing occasionally upon one of the wheels with a wooden bar, fearlessly rattles down the steep, and regulates his speed at pleasure. Having never seen any thing of the kind before, I was very much entertained with the various contrivances employed in the business of this place, and particularly with these self-impelled wagons rushing down the hill with an impetuosity that might have alarmed one a little, had it not been for the cool and careless faces of the helmsmen, some smoking their pipes, and others accompanying the rough music of the wheels with a song. On arriving at the South Pier, the wagons are pushed along it by men to any vessel receiving her freight, and are emptied with the utmost ease and expedition. Wooden stages are constructed at intervals along the pier, projecting over its side, with holes through them communicating with shoots beneath, which reach down nearly to the vessels' holds. The wagons are thrust out upon these stages, and having moveable bottoms which drop at the word of command, their whole contents are discharged in an instant. These machines are emphatically called *Hurries.*

The descent of wagons down the western hill has been simplified by a contrivance which saves the labour of forty men and as many horses. From the point where the declivity of the hill commences a regularly inclined plane has been cut, down which three wagons in a string roll at a time. The loaded wagons pull up three empty ones in their descent, but this counterpoise does not sufficiently reduce their speed, and they are therefore made to give motion to some machinery which requires considerable power, working a huge pair of bellows that force air through a valve into a receiver. As the receiver fills, more power is necessary for the depression of the bellows, and the wagons are thus duly checked as they acquire force in their descent. They are permitted, however, to roll down with considerable speed, and have a somewhat formidable look to a person meeting them, who is precluded by a bank on each side from getting more than a yard out of their way. A nervous man, I can conceive, might in the agitation of his useless precautions to avoid them, become entangled with them; but as they are confined to a certain tract by a rail-road, they could not possibly, even were the rope to break, get out of their way to run over him. A gentleman of the place told me that he once met them when they were running down with tremendous velocity, the people having forgotten to attach the rope to them; the sight, he said, was quite terrible, and a man not at all nervous might have trembled a little when he felt the ground shake as they thundered past him. A bulwark erected at the bottom prevented their doing any mischief beyond their own destruction; but when they struck against it, they were dashed to atoms, and the coals in them scattered away like dust.

The method of braking descending wagons on the incline was remarkable, but evidently successful, because in 1835 it was still in operation and noted by Sir George Head. He makes it quite clear that the incline drum then drove a two-cylinder air pump, and that control was exercised over speed by opening or closing the valve which exhausted the compressed air.

As we have seen, the railway was well known and well developed before the advent of mechanical power. But it remained a local phenomenon. Whether, if the locomotive had not come on the scene, a national network would have been built is an interesting question.

There were some enthusiasts for the idea and a few lines of some length intended for general freight transport outside mining areas were projected after 1800. Some of them were even built; the Surrey Iron Railway itself, from Wandsworth to Croydon, was one, although its extension to Merstham was mainly dependent on quarry business; one thinks also of the extraordinary granite-railed Hay Tor Tramroad, on Dartmoor. There was also the 24-mile Hay Railway of 1810, in Breconshire, and the 25-miles Plymouth & Dartmoor (again only partly interested in minerals), while the Stratford & Moreton, for instance, a 16-mile line opened in 1826, was intended to be part of a trunk route from London to Birmingham.

But as it happened, the locomotive came first. Steam power was applied first on the roads, in France by Cugnot in 1769 and in Britain by Murdoch in 1784; its first application on a railway was much later, and development of steam road vehicles was enthusiastically pursued by a devoted band of supporters up to the point where they could reasonably argue that they offered something better than the steam railway, and beyond (though they still argued). For on the railway steam power found a track that had been prepared for it; smooth, capable of bearing great weights without damage, with easy haulage and capacity for high speed. Best of all in some ways, it was a private way. A hue and cry could be raised against fiery monsters let loose on the public highroad, and their owners could be harassed through the law and by political pressure. But on the private railroad matters were otherwise; those were the days when the owner of land could keep politicians, and even the law, at some distance. It made all the difference. Whatever else might have happened, this was in fact the way that the railway became the national transport system after 1830.

CHAPTER TWO

The Beginning of Steam Power

Like interplanetary rocket flight, steam locomotion was an idea much in the public's mind many years before it actually happened. The power of steam was well appreciated in theory, just as people were aware of the potential of atomic power during the years between Rutherford, Einstein, and Hiroshima; the problem was, how to make use of it? And this was a question with two aspects. How could the thing be done, in mechanical detail; and was it worth doing as a commercial proposition? Unless the second question could be answered affirmatively, the first was of no more than academic importance.

James Watt, who was responsible for most of the improvements in steam engine design during the second half of the eighteenth century, and had brought steam power to the point where it was a practical proposition for stationary engines used both for mine pumping and for powering factory machinery, had a commanding position in the field, particularly as he was not only an inspired inventor but also an ultimately very wealthy businessman who (advised by Matthew Boulton) took good care to patent every idea he had on the subject. He did this whether he wished to develop the idea or not; and mobile steam engines were not an idea that he believed in. In his memoirs Watt wrote that, in company with a Dr Robison, he experimented with an expansion or high-pressure engine and described it in patents of 1769 and 1784, together with a mode of applying it to wheeled carriages; but he never actually built one. He had his reasons. The typical stationary engine was a condensing engine, using steam at a pressure of only 5–10 lb per square inch and deriving most of its power from atmospheric pressure on the piston after the steam in the cylinder had been condensed and a partial vacuum created; Watt's great innovation here was his invention of the separate condenser, which increased thermal efficiency by enabling the cylinder to be kept hot enough to avoid premature condensation, and so made it easier for some power to be developed by steam pressure on the return stroke. But with low pressure working, the cylinder had to be extremely large and bulky; and the separate condenser was even bigger and heavier again. The whole assembly was by no means portable.

An even stronger reason for Watt to reject steam locomotion was that, since for this reason of bulk it would involve the use of expansion engines rather than condensing engines, using steam at high pressure (25 lb per square inch at least), it was important that the boiler be capable of working safely. And boilers then were not really up to it. Cast iron pressure vessels are rather horrifying to contemplate, according to modern ideas; but cast iron was the only material available to make boilers with at the time. Cast iron tends to be brittle, and is subject to weaknesses caused by invisible flaws due to gas bubbles in the molten metal and the stresses of cooling unevenly in the mould; an altogether hideously unsuitable material, whose use in this context really implied the manufacture of steam bombs. One can imagine Watt's horror at the irresponsibility of this feckless Celt who proposed to set such a vessel on wheels and propel it down the highway, subjected to all the jolts and shocks of poor springing on rough and unmade surfaces, and charged with steam at the phenomenal pressure of 25 lb per square inch, talking glibly the while of higher pressures still. Watt was a sober man of affairs; his blood must have curdled at the thought. And there is no doubt that Trevithick was a man of absolutely the opposite temperament.

The first self-propelled vehicle was built and operated, once, by Nicholas Cugnot in Paris in 1769; it was a three-wheeled affair with the boiler suspended ahead of the single front wheel. It propelled itself, but not surprisingly having got a little way along the public road overturned, and Cugnot was dissuaded from continuing his experiments by the resulting uproar. The first steam-powered vehicle to run in Britain was built by a disobedient pupil of Watt's, William Murdoch, who in defiance of his master's orders built a model of the machine proposed in Watt's patent in 1784, and once again set it going along the road, this time causing no more than nervous damage.

The first railway locomotive was built by Richard Trevithick, and ran in 1804. Trevithick was the high priest of 'strong steam', and in

Cornwall had built a series of high-pressure pumping engines, working by expansion of steam in the cylinder and dispensing with the condenser; his practice was the antithesis of Watt's. But he built sufficiently strongly and well for his engines to be reliable, and this being so their smaller bulk (and therefore lower first cost) and greater fuel economy made them a more attractive commercial proposition. One of Trevithick's stationary engines now rests in the Science Museum at South Kensington, a dwarf between two rows of giant Watt and Newcomen-type beam engines, but producing the same horsepower. The sound engineering doctrines on which Watt rested his case thus began to seem less beyond challenge, and Trevithick's fame began to spread beyond his native Cornwall.

Emboldened by his success with stationary engines, Trevithick turned his attention to moving ones. With John Vivian, he patented his ideas in 1802, and then built two machines for use on roads; one was tried out later that year at Coalbrookdale and the other, a three-wheeler with rather better tracking and weight distribution than Cugnot's, was given an airing in the streets of London. They demonstrated the feasibility of the idea, but nothing was followed up, since there seemed to be no commercial case for it. The first locomotive to run on rails was in fact the result of a wager. Samuel Homfray, the South Wales ironmaster, had been sufficiently impressed with Trevithick's plans to buy a half share in his patent, and laid a bet with one of his colleagues that a steam engine could be made to haul a 10-ton load over the 9½-mile Penydaren Tramway, recently built to connect the Penydaren Ironworks near Merthyr with the canal at Abercynon.

The wager duly signed and sealed, the 33-year-old Trevithick set to and built a locomotive, as nearly as possible one of his stationary engines mounted on wheels. The cast iron boiler contained a U-shaped return flue, so that the chimney was next to the firedoor, and a single cylinder, 8¼ inch diameter by 54 inch stroke, was mounted centrally in the boiler and above the flue. The piston drove a crosshead consisting of a bar which spanned the width of the entire machine, and by means of connecting rods mounted at each end drove a flywheel 8 feet in diameter, running on a shaft attached to the other end of the boiler. It was very definitely a Mark I device; its operation was perilous in the extreme, as to tend the fire in motion it was necessary to crouch down below the piston-rod and crosshead, which were banging to and fro on their 4½-foot stroke. Nevertheless, it went. In an effort to quieten the blast Trevithick turned the exhaust steam up the chimney, and at once observed the effect this had on the fire; the harder the engine worked, the greater the draught induced in the chimney and so through the grate, and the hotter the fire would burn. It is also clear that Trevithick appreciated that sufficient traction, at any rate for the limited purpose intended, would be obtained from the adhesion of plain iron wheels on a plain iron surface, and that there was no need for a rack or any similar device.

The earliest records we have of the running of this first locomotive are two letters written by Trevithick himself, to Davies Giddy, who was later President of the Royal Society. On 15 February 1804 he wrote:

> Last Saturday we lighted the fire in the tram-waggon and worked it without the wheels to try the engine. On Monday we put it on the tramroad. It worked very well, and ran uphill and down with great ease, and was very manageable. We had plenty of steam and power . . . The bet will not be determined until the middle of next week.

On 20 February he wrote again:

> The tram-waggon has been at work several times. It works exceedingly well, and is much more manageable than horses. We have not tried to draw more than 10 tons at a time, but I doubt not we could draw 40 tons at a time very well; 10 tons stands no chance at all with it. We have been but two miles on the road and back again, and shall not go further until Mr Homfray comes home. . . . The engine, with water included, is about 5 tons. It runs up the tramroad of 2 inches in a yard [i.e. up a grade of 1 in 18, presumably on some siding] at 40 strokes per minute with the empty waggons. The engine moves forward 9 feet at every stroke. [Hence its speed was just under 5 mph on this grade.] . . . The steam that is discharged from the engine is turned up the chimney about 3 feet above the fire, and when the engine works 40 strokes a minute not the smallest particle of steam appears out of the top of the chimney. . . . I think it is made a fixed air by the heat of the chimney. The fire burns much better when the steam goes up the chimney than

> when the engine is idle. I intend to make a smaller engine for the road, as this has much more power than is wanted here. This engine is to work a hammer. . . . We shall continue our journey on the road today with the engine until we meet Mr Homfray and the London engineer, and intend to take the horses out of their coach, fasten it to the engine, and draw them home.

Unfortunately there is no record of whether this first passenger train ever ran in fact, but the 10ton load to win the wager was certainly worked down the line the following day, Tuesday, 21 February.

The Penydaren Tramway was a 4 ft 2 in plateway 9½ miles long. From Penydaren to Abercynon, in the direction of the trial, it fell 340 feet, on an average grade of about 1 in 145 but with short stretches of 1 in 50. So in fact the duty Trevithick's engine had to perform to win Homfray's bet for him was not unduly onerous, as is proved by the fact that according to the record Trevithick did not need to put any more water in the boiler. The run was performed in 4 hours 5 minutes; there were several delays because the cast iron tramplates sometimes broke under the engine's weight, and in one place the line had to be slewed under a bridge to give sufficient clearance for the chimney. Local tradition has it that the engine was towed back uphill to the works by road; certainly it was very soon dismounted and used to drive a hammer in the works, as Trevithick had intended.

At this distance of time, it all looks rather like a publicity stunt, designed to develop interest in the idea, rather than convert the Penydaren line to steam power at once. Unfortunately, on 6 March Homfray met with an accident driving a gig and was incapacitated for a while; this seems to have spoilt the plans. Trevithick did indeed receive an order, from Blackett of Wylam, for another locomotive, built in 1805; this was basically very similar to the earlier machine, but with the important difference that the cylinder, with its murderous trombone-slide arrangement, was placed at the front end of the boiler, away from the firedoor; thus it would not have been the fireman but a tardy trespasser who might have been picked up and shaken to death. But this engine never ran at Wylam; possibly because he knew it would be too heavy for his track, Blackett rejected it and it was found employment driving some machinery. Trevithick's third and final locomotive, the *Catch-me-who-can*, built in

1808, was another venture into publicity; it was an improved machine, still with only one cylinder, but this mounted vertically and driving directly on to the wheels, with no flywheel. It operated on a circular track near the top of Gower Street, close to the present Euston station, in London, for a month, selling joyrides at a shilling a time; a broken rail finally closed the show. Public interest was developed all right, and Rowlandson made a famous engraving of the scene, but no commercial proposals came of it.

After these disappointments, Trevithick gave up locomotives, and turned his somewhat fickle attention elsewhere, including a catastrophic mining venture in South America. He was the pioneer, the man of imagination; and like so many of that sort, he was not dogged enough to stay the course, and in the end therefore failed. He died in 1833, and his obituary in the *Civil Engineers' and Architects' Journal* said:

> Trevithick began better than Stephenson; he had friends in Cornwall and London, and he ought not to have left Stephenson to work out the locomotive engine and the railway. Trevithick was always unhappy and unlucky; always beginning something new, and never ending what he had in hand. The world ever went wrong with him, he said; but in truth he always went wrong with the world. The world would have done enough for him, had he chosen to make a right use of any one thing. He found a partner for his high-pressure engine; he built a locomotive; he had orders for others; he sent one to Wylam, which like most things in which he had a hand was so wretchedly made that it was put to other uses. . . . No one thing did well. All were afraid, and at length no-one would have anything to do with him.

The first locomotives to be a commercial success were those placed in service on the Middleton Railway, at Leeds, in 1812. The economic case for them was assisted by the fact that due to the Napoleonic Wars the price of food in general and grain in particular had increased very greatly, and this had the result of making the maintenance of a stock of horses for railway haulage extremely expensive. Concerned to reduce this cost, several mineowners decided that the time had come to take the idea of locomotives seriously. But the technical improvements made at the same time were very considerable indeed.

The achievement of Matthew Murray, of the firm of Fenton, Murray and Wood, who was responsible for their construction, has been somewhat obscured by the fact that the Middleton Railway used Blenkinsop's rack-and-pinion system, which proved to be an evolutionary dead end. John Blenkinsop of Leeds was the agent of the Tyneside coalowner Charles Brandling, and managed the Middleton collieries, also Brandling's property, on his behalf. Blenkinsop believed, with many others at that time, that the grip of a smooth iron wheel on an iron rail would not in practice be sufficient to enable a locomotive to haul a worthwhile load. This was a more reasonable view than it now seems to be. At the time little was known about the rolling resistance of railway vehicles, as we have seen, and the need to produce a light engine that would not overload the cast iron rails was paramount. It was also the intention to have an engine that could haul a considerable load, even if only at a very low speed, and for this a rack was certainly essential. Like many controversies of railway history, this one has been obscured by clouds and fogs of special pleading: the fact that it was later found practical to move at speeds greater than two or three miles an hour, making the haulage of a lighter load an economic proposition and avoiding the need to provide for brute drawbar pull to the same extent, has been overlooked. Blenkinsop was a better engineer in his turn than is often admitted now. Much has been written about how the partisans of the Blenkinsop system claimed that a smooth-wheeled locomotive would not even be able to move its own weight, but would sit still with its wheels slithering round helplessly; certainly some of the armchair enthusiasts said such things; but anybody with practical experience of railway operation even then must have known that *some* adhesion would be obtained without a rack. But the well-known uncertainties of braking on smooth rails in wet weather with horse-drawn wagons lent weight to the question, would this be enough?

The Middleton Railway, therefore, was relaid in 1811–12, with cast iron edge rails on Blenkinsop's patent, which had rack teeth cast into the outside of one rail only. Blenkinsop had wanted both rails to have the rack, but this was refused him on the grounds of expense. A central rack rail, which would at least have been a symmetrical arrangement, was impossible because of the need to keep the space between the rails free for horses. Matthew Murray at the same time built two locomotives to run on the line, and the fact that

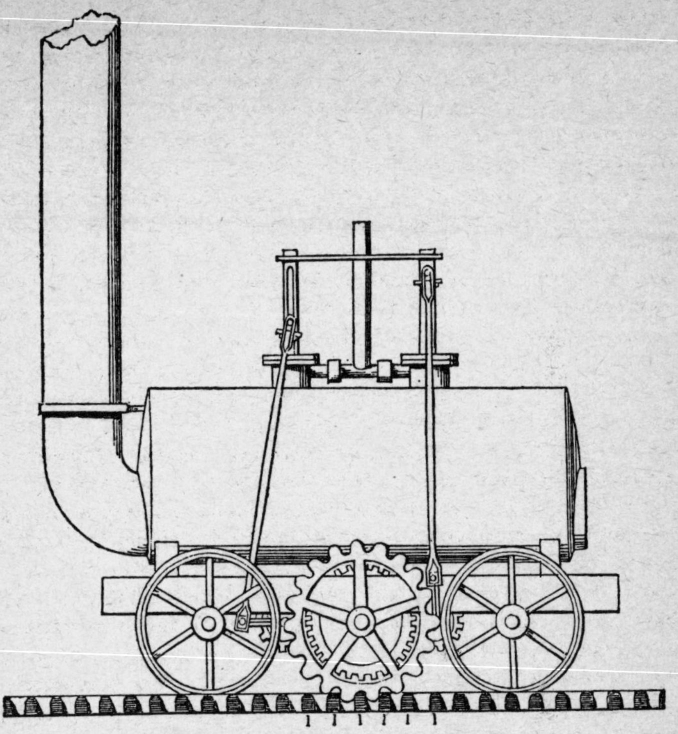

Figure 1 A Blenkinsop type locomotive

two were ordered, rather than a timid experimental one, showed that Blenkinsop meant business. They followed Trevithick's designs in many particulars, and Trevithick was paid a fee for the use of his patent rights; but Murray's engines showed several important advances over Trevithick's practice. First of all, there were two cylinders; both still set into the boiler, and driving vertically in the manner of Trevithick's London engine, but giving a much smoother drive than a single cylinder. The vertical connecting rods drove two crankshafts, one for each cylinder, which were connected by gearing to a central shaft with the single rack wheel attached at one end. The workmanship of the engines was sound enough to ensure their success; the *Prince Regent* and *Salamanca* began regular work on 12

August 1812, following trials; they were joined a year later by two more similar machines, and between them these four worked the Middleton line for the next thirty years. Weighing five tons, they proved capable at the start of hauling a load of 94 tons, at 3½ mph, which Blenkinsop claimed enabled each engine to do the work of sixteen horses.

They did, however, show some curious regressions from Trevithick's practice. First of all, the boiler was of the single straight flue type, which although easier to manufacture than Trevithick's return flue had much less heating surface, and therefore a lower steam-raising capacity as well as a higher fuel consumption. Secondly, at first the exhaust steam was not sent up the chimney, but released straight to the atmosphere. So Blenkinsop's engines were originally shortwinded, having to stop from time to time to allow pressure to recover; still, on a line only 3½ miles in length this did not matter too much. It seems likely that they were later modified and given blast-pipes; possibly they outlived the rack rail, and were rebuilt to drive through the carrying wheels in the normal way, using a train of gears, since Nicholas Wood in the 1838 edition of his *Treatise on Railroads* remarks: 'By the use of the rack rail, Mr Blenkinsop's engine was enabled to ascend acclivities, which Mr Trevithick's engine, from want of adhesion, could not surmount. . . . But it having since been proved, that the adhesion of the wheels was sufficient, to accomplish the progressive motion, the rack-rail has been abandoned.' On the other hand, Wood may not have meant to imply that it had been abandoned at Middleton: Sir George Head's *Home Tour* describes the railway as it was in 1835, when the rack was certainly still used.

But the deed was done, and the fact that steam locomotives were in service and justifying themselves commercially, on however short and obscure a railway, was a powerful incentive for further development. Two more similar engines, also built by Murray, were placed in service on the Kenton & Coxlodge line, near Newcastle, in 1813, but these were less successful and were taken out of use two years later. Another two locomotives of Blenkinsop pattern were built at the Royal Iron Foundry in Berlin in 1816 and 1818, but neither saw useful service.

Two other engineers were working on locomotives at about the same time, and both addressed themselves especially to the traction problem, while trying out different methods from Blenkinsop's rack. William and Edward Chapman patented a machine in 1812 which is sufficiently well described by Wood.

> The locomotion of the engine was effected by means of a chain, stretched along the middle of the railroad. . . . This chain was made to wind partly round, or to pass over, a grooved wheel, turned by the engine, of such a form that the wheel could not turn round without causing the chain to pass along with it. . . . At intervals of every eight or ten yards, the chain was secured, by means of upright forks, into which it fell, when left at liberty. . . . The chain was prevented from slipping, when the grooved wheel was turned round, by friction rollers pressing it into the groove. Mr Chapman had one of his engines tried upon the Heaton railroad, near Newcastle, but it was soon abandoned; the great friction of the chain, and also its liability to get out of order, operated considerably against it.

What Wood does not add is that Chapman also patented the idea of supporting an engine on eight or more wheels, by means of bogies, thus spreading the weight and saving damage to the track. He built a second locomotive in 1814, which had two four-wheeled bogies, all wheels being driven by a system of gearing which allowed for the relative movement of bogies and frames; this was clearly an adhesion engine, although it was also fitted with a chain wheel. Chapman's intention by then was to use chain haulage only on certain steep sections of line. This seems never to have been done in regular service, probably because the complications of picking up the chain and threading it through beneath the engine at the foot of the hill were too great.

A considerably more extraordinary machine was patented in 1813 by William Brunton, of the Butterley Ironworks, near Derby, and tried out in 1815. This had a single-flue boiler with a single horizontal cylinder mounted above the firedoor, regressing to the Penydaren engine in this respect; but the cylinder did not drive any wheels, it drove two legs. It was a remarkable example of misplaced ingenuity; just as early designers of flying machines thought that it would be necessary to imitate the action of birds and provide men with flapping wings, so Brunton felt that the locomotive had to imitate the action of the carthorse. The two legs were provided with 'feet', complete with anklejoints, and a system of levers, ratchets, and straps was provided so that each stroke of the piston drove one leg back and returned the other forward, lifted clear of the ground meanwhile. The machine weighed only 2¼ tons, and was found on trial to develop 6 horsepower at 2½ mph; but it suffered from the drawback that it had to propel its train, to allow the legs freedom of movement, and was non-reversible. Horses would therefore still have had to be used in one direction, unless a loop was put in at each terminal. However, the engine blew up on its trials, killing its crew and several spectators, and put paid to further developments.

Christopher Blackett, the owner of the Wylam colliery, near Newcastle, and his manager William Hedley were responsible for the second group of locomotives to be a commercial success. The Wylam Railway, from the colliery to the Tyne at Lemington, five miles away, had been relaid in 1808, with cast iron tramplates replacing the original wooden rails; but it was still a difficult line to work as it had some lengths where the gradient was against the load. As a result, the expense of horse haulage was a particular burden, and Blackett was forced to consider locomotives as an alternative to closing the pit.

Hedley was a methodical engineer, and was not convinced that there was any need for rack rails and the like; and he deserves credit for testing this issue first by proper experiment before committing himself to the final construction. About 1811 he built a light wagon, consisting of a framework on which men could stand while turning cranks that drove the wheels; the weight of the wagon could be varied by attaching ballast. By this means he was able to determine exactly how much tractive effort could be obtained through smooth wheels with different adhesive weights bearing on them; and finding the load haulage capacity of a given drawbar pull at the same time, he was able to build a smooth-wheeled locomotive in full confidence that it would do all that was required of it. His first, tried in February 1813, was capable of hauling a train, but not of giving effective service; his second, which first ran in May of the same year, was wholly successful.

Writing in 1836, Hedley stated:

> The [first] Engine had one Cylinder and a Flywheel; it went badly, the obvious defect being want of Steam. Another Engine

> was then constructed, the Boiler was of Malleable Iron, the tube containing the Fire was enlarged, and in place of passing directly through the Boiler into the Chimney, it was made to return again through the Boiler to the Chimney, at the same end of the Boiler as the Fire-place was. This was a most important improvement. The Engine was placed upon four wheels and went well; a short time after it commenced it regularly drew eight loaded Coal Waggons after it, at the rate of from four to five miles per hour on the Wylam Railroad which was in a very bad State . . . it is needless to pursue the subject further than to state that for a length of Time each new Engine went better and took more Waggons than its Predecessor.

Three similar engines appear to have been built, and acquired probably unofficial names: *Puffing Billy* (now at the Science Museum, South Kensington), *Wylam Dilly* (now at the Edinburgh Museum), and *Lady Mary*.

Hedley's biographer Mark Archer, writing in 1882, states that the return-flue boiler carried steam at 50 lb per square inch. The two cylinders drove vertically upwards, but not in the same way as at Middleton; for the first time, they were not set inside the boiler, but one on each side of it, at the opposite end to the firedoor. The cylinders drove two beams, whose fulcrum was a rigid pivot behind the chimney, and which in turn actuated connecting rods driving a shaft set below the frames and centrally between the wheels, to which motion was again transmitted by gears. Hedley had clearly studied the Middleton locomotives, and had improved on them in two major respects apart from dispensing with the rack; he used the return-flue boiler with its superior performance, and he concentrated the drive on to one shaft. On the Middleton engines each cylinder drove a separate shaft, so that alternate power strokes were delivered to opposite ends of the gear train, which must have caused considerable grinding and gnashing and additional wear and tear, especially considering the limited accuracy with which gears could at that time be cut.

On the other hand, in its original form the engine was too heavy for the plate rails, and had at once to be modified; it seems that the the other two were similarly altered during construction. Hedley made use of Chapman's patent and set the engine on bogies, which allowed it to be used successfully since the axleload was halved. On the other hand, the engraving published in Wood's book (plate 4) shows that the conversion was achieved by lifting the original frame bodily above the two bogie pivots, so that the drive had to be transmitted from the original jackshaft to a king pinion held in an A-frame beneath it, from whence the gears on each bogie were driven, the relative movement of the bogies being accommodated, one assumes sufficiently (most of the time), by allowing the gears to float independently while hoping that they stayed in mesh. The whole thing was something of a mechanical faux pas, and Wood's engraving, perhaps mischievously, shows the gears on the verge of disengagement. However, the arrangement evidently sufficed. There has been some controversy as to whether the bogies actually pivoted, but their separate framing surely argues that they did, or were intended to. About 1830 the Wylam line was converted from a plateway to a five-foot gauge railway, and the *Puffing Billies* were therefor restored to their original four-wheeled condition; they remained in action until the line was again converted, this time to standard gauge, in 1862.

A number of other modifications are evident from a comparison of the 1825 engraving with an 1862 photograph, although surprisingly few. One is that the beams were altered, the original rigid pivot, which involved the use of a floating link between the piston rod and the free end of the beam, being replaced by the more complicated but easier to maintain Watt parallel motion (much used with stationary engines). The piston rod was guided in a straight line by the beam, which was in turn controlled by a link connecting its midpoint with a fulcrum (supported by a diagonal strut) above the cylinder. Link and beam moved like scissors. The other change is that the rather intriguing 1825 two-wheeled tender, supporting a water barrel and attached by a rigid coupling to the bogie frame, gave way to a rather less unconventional four-wheeled tender. Coal and water supplies in both cases were very limited, with coal carried on a mere tray about four feet square.

Another difference was in the exhaust arrangements. At first Hedley passed the waste steam into a silencer, in an effort to cut down the apparently rather objectionable noise made by the Middleton engines; this was only partially successful, so that in a further attempt to quieten the panting which gave Hedley's engines their name in folklore the exhaust was led on from the silencer into the chimney, where of course it was found to have the encouraging action on the fire that had been noted ten years earlier by Trevithick, and which was not employed at Middleton. By 1862 the silencer had disappeared completely.

One other incident in the history of the *Wylam Dillies* is recorded by Archer; in 1822 there was a keelmen's strike in the River Tyne, which succeeded for a while in bringing the transport of coal downstream to a halt. Hedley thereupon mounted one of his engines in a boat, attaching paddlewheeles to the jackshaft, and with the resulting tugboat steamed through the angry picketline on the banks with a number of coal barges in tow. The locomotive stayed in this marine employment for some six months after the strike had been broken.

If one asks the average schoolboy 'who invented the locomotive?' the reply will almost certainly be 'George Stephenson'; but it was not until this stage that Stephenson comes into the story. Born in 1781, he was already a man with a solid record of achievement as an enginewright and mechanic, and had just been appointed to be in charge of all the machinery in the collieries of the 'Grand Allies', the partnership which had obtained a commanding position in the Northumberland coal industry and controlled the largest number of collieries there. His responsibilities were therefore many, and covered a much wider field than transport; indeed, he has a secondary claim to fame as the inventor of the first practical miner's safety lamp, simultaneously with Sir Humphry Davy. However, in 1813 the Grand Allies, having observed the progress that others were making in locomotive design and not wishing to be left behind, instructed Stephenson to build one for their Killingworth railway, north of Newcastle. Stephenson had previously been the enginewright at this pit, working alongside Nicholas Wood, who later became Viewer (or Manager) there.

Stephenson's first locomotive, the *Blucher*, first ran in July 1814. She was a very close copy of the Middleton engines, with the main difference that she dispensed with the rack; the drive was taken by gears to the carrying wheels. In particular, she had the straight-flue boiler, and waste steam was exhausted directly to the air. She also had a long train of gears; longer than the Middleton engines, since the central wheel ran only on an idle shaft, and two additional wheels were needed to drive the main axles. So the wear and tear caused by the divided nature of the drive was correspondingly increased.

Quite apart from any question of his native genius, Stephenson had an advantage simply because he worked for a powerful employer with large resources; and during the next twelve years or so he was responsible for the building of no fewer than sixteen locomotives at Killingworth and in Newcastle. This gave him the opportunity to make several improvements as time went on, even though he remained faithful throughout to the single-flue boiler. This was admittedly wasteful, but when coal was so cheap at the pithead that the poorer grades were used as railway ballast, this hardly mattered much; the important point was that it was cheaper to build than the Trevithick type, and Stephenson found that its steamraising capacity could be improved sufficiently for the short runs performed by increasing the diameter of the flue.

Stephenson's first improvement, applied to his second engine, the *Wellington*, consisted of dispensing with the train of gears used in every locomotive before then, except Brunton's and Trevithick's third. As Wood writes, 'the communication of the pressure upon the piston to the travelling wheels by the cogwheels produced great noise, and in some parts of the stroke considerable jerks, and when the teeth became at all worn caused a rattling noise. . . . To obviate this became desirable, and Mr Stephenson, in conjunction with Mr Dodd [the Head Viewer at Killingworth] took out a patent for a method of communicating the power of the engine directly to the wheels'. This was in February 1815. The method was simply to apply the connecting rods directly to the 'travelling wheels', by means of a crankpin set into the wheel casting; the complication which then arose was that with the abolition of the gearing, the wheels were no longer coupled, and so since each cylinder drove those above which it was set, some means of keeping their motion alternating at 90° had to be devised. The 1815 patent prescribed two alternatives. One was the use of a single inside coupling rod, running on cranked axles; not surprisingly, no engine to this design was built, since quite apart from the difficulty of making crank axles, one coupling rod on its own is of course useless as it is powerless at the end of its stroke and can easily become crossed and jammed. The other method patented was the use of what Wood describes as a 'peculiar sort of endless chain' running on sprocket wheels; this seems an obvious enough expedient to us, but in fact it was the very first appearance of the type of chain now familiar to us on bicycles, which owes its origin to the *Wellington*. This chain drive remained in use for some years and gave satisfactory service; it was however necessary to enable one pair of wheels to be moved outwards to allow for the chain stretching, until it had lengthened sufficiently to make it possible to remove one complete link.

It was not until some years later that the even simpler and more elegant method of using two coupling rods was adopted instead. The reason for this was probably one of manufacture; since the connecting rod crankpins at opposite *ends* of the engine had to be maintained at rightangles to each other, while the same was necessary for the coupling rod crankpins on opposite *sides*, the phases were inconsistent on two of the four wheels and it was necessary therefore to use a return crank on these, giving the coupling rod a second pin outside and in the correct position, while allowing clearance for the connecting rod and pin inside. The stress on such a return crank at each stroke would be considerable, and it was necessary first to devise a method of keying the whole assembly to the wheel which was sufficiently strong.

Stephenson's second improvement was concerned with suspension. All previous locomotives had been unsprung, and it was not then possible to make springs sufficiently strong, or stiff enough to resist the rolling action created by the working of vertical cylinders at each side. This lack of springing certainly exacerbated the rail-breakage problem. Stephenson's answer was the 'steam spring', in which the axles ran in bearings attached to the ends of piston rods protruding from cylinders let into the bottom of the boiler. When the engine was cold, the bearings rested on the frames and the engine 'rode solid'; but when steam was up the bearings were forced downwards and so some element of elasticity was given to the suspension. This was a complicated arrangement, and must have caused a maintenance problem; but it was used on most Stephenson locomotives from 1816 until, in the early 1820s, adequately strong laminated plate springs were produced.

With these improvements, Stephenson had a machine that was reasonably sound mechanically and capable of moving a great deal faster than walking pace without doing itself injury. He experimented somewhat with the steam blast, but with a single-flue boiler,

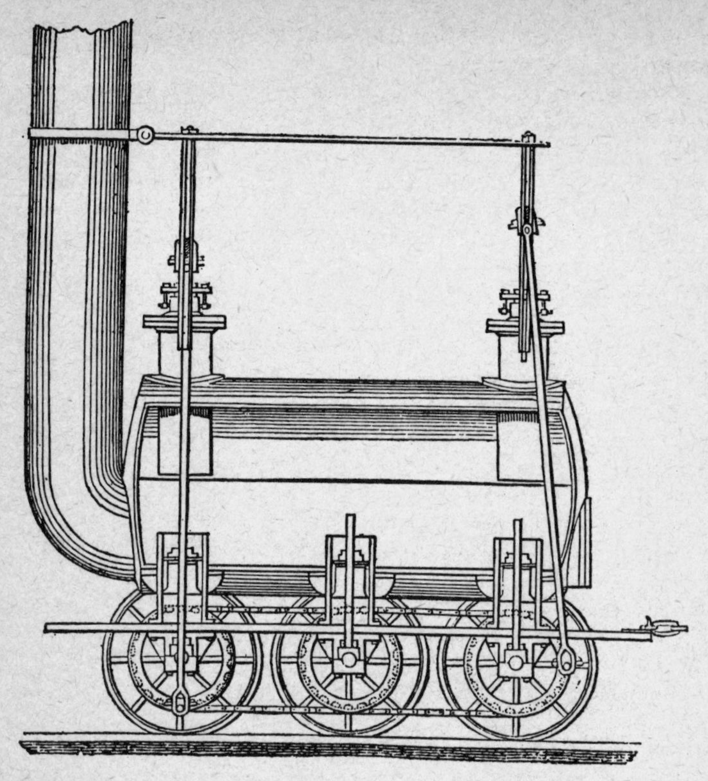

Figure 2 The six-wheeled version of the early Stephenson locomotive, with chain coupling and steam springs, as built for the Kilmarnock & Troon line

its advantage in freer steam production was not great and was countered by the increased coal consumption and throwing of the fire out of the chimney. Locomotives began to be an accepted part of the everyday Tyneside scene, doing a customary task, and they began to be built for railways rather further afield. One that Stephenson built for the plateway between Kilmarnock and Troon in 1817 was interesting, as it was an 0–6–0, with all wheels coupled by chain drive and provided with steam springs. But generally they were all, except for Hedley's and Blenkinsop's, of one standard outline, with a vertical cylinder set near each end of a single-flue boiler, and the four wheels coupled by chains or rods.

One item which needed considerable attention was valves and valvegear. Trevithick had used two rotary plug valves, working on the same principle as the primitive tap in a beer barrel. In one position these admitted steam to one end of the cylinder and opened the other to exhaust, and when turned through 90° they reversed these openings. These plugs were operated by a long rod visible in drawings of the engines, which had two collars struck at either end of the stroke (and thus moved to the opposite position) by a fork attached to the piston rod. The movement of the valve was therefore only a few degrees in advance of the piston, live steam entered the cylinder for almost the whole length of the stroke (or in other words the 'cut-off' was nearly 100 per cent), and the expansive properties of the steam were wasted. A handle attached to the end of the valve rod made it possible to set the valve at starting for movement in either direction.

Matthew Murray was responsible for the introduction of the slide valve, which was perhaps his greatest contribution to locomotive design (see plate 10). This is a single D-shaped casting moved to and fro across a flat surface containing two slots, or 'ports', each communicating with one end of the cylinder, with a third slot leading to the exhaust lying between them. The outside of the 'D' is surrounded with high-pressure steam from the boiler, and when one port is uncovered this can enter the cylinder and drive the piston. But when this happens, the other port is opened to the inside of the 'D', allowing waste steam to escape to the exhaust. The great advantages of the slide valve are that it is simpler to operate and easier to keep steamtight; it is possible to provide much larger passages for steam, and it is also possible, although the advantages of doing so were discovered later by practical experience, to arrange for a delay during which both the admission and the exhaust ports are closed, allowing steam to work expansively in the cylinder. Since this is done by increasing the width of the flat face at each end of the 'D' so that it overlaps each side of the port fairly considerably, this is called the 'lap' of the valve. It is not certain that Murray's valves had any significant amount of lap; but it is clear that Stephenson's did, though not perhaps at first.

Originally these slide valves were driven by an arrangement of collared rods similar to Trevithick's, throwing the valve across to the opposite position just as the piston reached the end of its stroke. Stephenson's locomotives, however, had an improved system. It is not clear whether it was fitted to the *Blucher*, as no drawing survives of this machine, but certainly the valves of the later Killingworth locomotives were driven by eccentrics, a step forward that was due to Nicholas Wood. One eccentric was mounted on each axle, and each drove its valve through rods and bell crank; but the significant change brought about by using eccentrics was that for the first time it became possible to arrange for the valve to be moved while the piston was still some way from the end of its stroke. In conjunction with the use of lapped valves, this meant that it was now possible to cut off the admission of steam to the cylinder at some point during the stroke, and thus to obtain a great economy by allowing it to expand while still driving the piston, before the exhaust port opened. The degree of expansion attainable depended on the fixed setting of the collars on the eccentric rod, and was not under the control of the driver; it could not be reduced to allow a cut-off much less than about 60 per cent as this would lead to a risk of getting inescapably stuck on dead centre when attempting to start. But Wood describes experiments with one locomotive to determine the most economical amount of lap and point of cut-off by means of movable collars, and presumably the most favourable setting found was then standardized.

The eccentrics used were 'slip eccentrics', which moved by themselves from forward to reverse position on the axle when the engine changed its direction. But this meant that it was necessary for the engine actually to move the opposite way for a yard or so, to allow the eccentrics to take up their new position. In order to avoid the need to use a horse or a crowbar for this purpose, the valves could be set by hand into a correct starting position by moving the arm of the bell crank along the free travel of the eccentric rod; however this would have been a rather skilful and chancy business that must have done something to separate the men from the boys.

Other details changed too; some changed little. Some drawings show boiler barrels unclad, though this must have led to considerable heat loss and it was an easy matter carried out in most cases to lag the boiler, or at least the cylindrical part of it, in a simple wooden jacket. Safety valves were all of the weighted lever type, all too

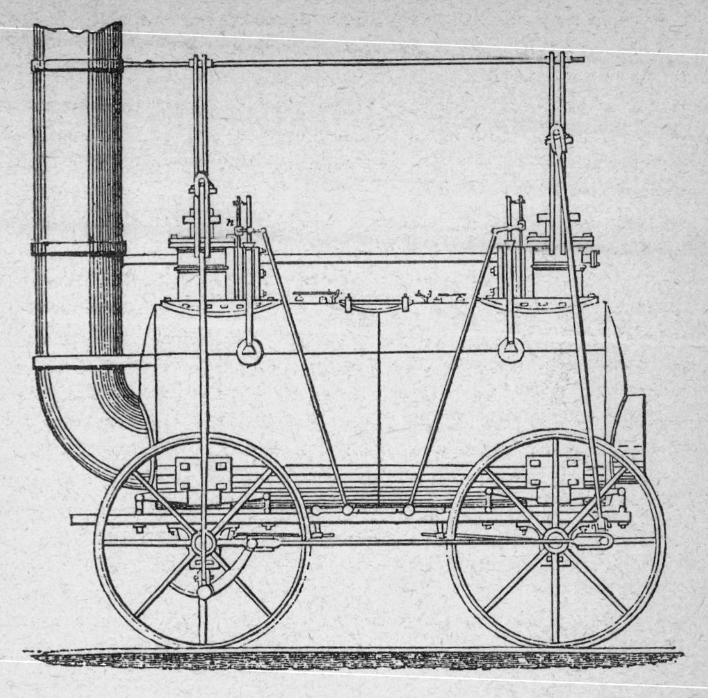

Figure 3 Stephenson's Killingworth locomotive, as modified by Wood, with coupling rods, slip eccentrics, and plate springs

easily held down by the overenthusiastic engine man. And every locomotive since Penydaren has had a basically similar design of fusible plug; a screwed brass plug set into the arch of the firetube, or crown of the fire box, with a lead core which will melt if the water level falls to uncover it and so give warning of the danger of explosion by releasing a jet of steam into the fire. It is by no means a foolproof gadget; if poorly maintained, the lead core may become encrusted with scale strong enough to hold the pressure after melting has taken place, while of course it is essential that the enginemen should notice that the plug has in fact 'dropped', which might not be easy if the engine is working hard. Most boiler explosions (and the last one on British railways occurred near Wrexham as recently as the mid-1950s) have been due to neglect of the fusible plug's warning; but the device has prevented countless others.

There was already considerable talk about railways and tramroads, and the possibility of some day establishing a network of these to cover the country; as we have seen, after 1815 some ambitious horse-powered lines were projected, and some actually built. The commercial success of steam locomotives, although still on a small and local scale, caused some to wonder whether they could be developed to fill this larger need. One of the first publicists of the idea of the Steam Railway was Thomas Gray of Nottingham, whose book *Observations on a General Iron Rail-way* was first published in 1820. Gray was a tremendous enthusiast, but clearly not a very considerable engineer. The frontispiece of his book is an engraving showing three trains, one passenger and two freight, hauled by Blenkinsop-type locomotives complete with rack drive, but lacking any tenders or coal and water supply; as at Middleton, the exhaust steam passes straight to the atmosphere. Each is driven by a happy-looking individual in a top hat, perched on a curlicue and unsafe-looking seat within an inch or two of the firedoor. Each train has three vehicles, and each vehicle a brakesman or attendant, some gaily blowing coachmens' horns; the rather grander passenger coaches have two attendants each, and two compartments, as well as luggage on the roof and passengers 'outside' as on stagecoaches. A dedicatory verse on the title page reads:

> No speed with this, can swiftest horse compare;
> No weight like this, canal or vessel bear.
> As this will commerce every way promote
> To this, let sons of commerce grant their vote.

In the book, Gray prints maps of the national railway network he envisaged; they are not particularly practical routes from the engineering point of view, but laid out to cater for the major flows of trade, and thus essentially a system of lines radiating from London. He expected that the important routes would have six-track lines, which certainly shows largeness of thought; but he believed in the necessity of Blenkinsop's rack and his ideas of the capacity of locomotives at that time were strangely wide of the mark. 'One steam engine', he wrote, 'on an *improved plan*, would draw from London to Edinburgh three stage-coaches, each carrying twice the number of passengers of ordinary stages, in 30 hours, which now require 300 horses and at least 50 hours' time.' The full title of his book was *Observations on a General Iron Rail-way, or Land Steam Conveyance; to supersede the necessity of Horses in all Public Vehicles? showing its Vast Superiority in Every Respect, over all the present Pitiful Methods of Conveyance by Turnpike Roads, Canals, and Coasting-Traders.*

Gray was regarded by his contemporaries as rather a figure of fun. Writing in 1851 John Francis says of him:

> He used to be noted for what was considered a whimsical crotchet, namely, that a general system of iron railways might and ought to be laid down, on which trains of carriages drawn by locomotive steam engines should run, and thus supercede the use of coaches, and also, in a great measure, canal boats and stage waggons for goods. This scheme, it was said, had for years completely taken possession of and absorbed Mr Gray's whole mind; it was the one great and incessant subject of his thoughts and conversation; begin where you would, on whatever subject, the weather, the news, politics, it would not be many minutes before you would be enveloped with steam, listening to a harangue on a general iron railway. Of course Thomas Gray was looked on as little better than a madman, a dreamer, a builder of castles in the air, one of the race of discoverers of the elixir of life, the philosopher's stone, perpetual motion. With one consent he was voted an intolerable bore.

An interesting quotation these days. Gray was, of course, vindicated by events, in a manner which he must have found very satisfying. But one wonders what his shade would feel now, when the wheel has turned so full a circle. Certainly the railway scene these days has on its fringes any number of enthusiasts whom Francis's description fits like a glove.

CHAPTER THREE

The Locomotive and its Rivals

Between 1813 and 1815 there was, as we have seen, something of a burst in the rate of steam locomotive development. But some lean years followed. Between 1814 and 1826 only one man in Britain, George Stephenson, built any locomotives. During all that time, travelling engines were being used on the Middleton, Wylam, and Killingworth railways, and on these short runs for specialized traffic where speed was of little account they were proving their technical feasibility, and little by little they were building up a case for their economic feasibility too. But the second took much longer. In those days there were no kindly government subsidies and grants in aid of desperate or limping enterprises, and an entrepreneur had to raise money on commercial terms (or dip into his own pocket) to find capital to develop a new invention; there was a great deal more caution than we are used to nowadays in such matters. It was one thing to show that locomotives could pull trains; but quite another to prove that they paid, and not even the experience of a year or two would convince the man of business that this was so. Admittedly one could by then begin to get some idea of running costs, but what about depreciation and renewals? There was no experience yet to answer the question, 'How long will such a machine remain serviceable if only this amount of money is spent on its repairs?' The only way to find out the answer was to wait and see. The somewhat shrill arguments of Thomas Gray did not affect the issue during these years.

It is impossible now to know the truth, but one suspects that behind each of the three railways using locomotives stood an owner with a long pocket, who had enough faith in the invention to pay the bills during the trials and tribulations of development; and surely we only know half of these. Certainly we can name the owners; Charles Brandling (who also had interests on Tyneside) at

Middleton; Christopher Blackett at Wylam; and the Grand Allies, the group formed by the Liddell, Montague, and Bower families, who were the biggest coalowners in the north-east, and who were the backers of Stephenson. It would be very surprising if the figures of cost per ton-mile that began to be quoted, showing a saving over horse haulage, were not originally compiled on a basis of 'well actually it cost a bit more, but if we had done thus and so we could have avoided such and such'. This is, of course, perfectly legitimate so long as the qualification is a just one; the extra costs have to be written down to experience. But the money still had to be found. There is nothing puzzling about the pause in progress; the locomotive partisans were gaining experience, and the commercial community were very properly letting them and their financial backers get on with it. Besides which, Waterloo had been fought, the war was over, and it seemed reasonable to hope that the price of corn would now fall and the maintenance of a stock of horses would become less costly. In fact, this did not happen; but it was not for some years that it became clear that it would not, and this also helped to explain the reawakening of interest in steam haulage.

We have seen how Stephenson's locomotives were developed during the ten years between the *Blucher* and the founding of Robert Stephenson & Co. in 1823. They remained basically the same, with a single-flue boiler and two vertical cylinders mounted centrally in the boiler and above each axle; but coupling the wheels by chains was soon superseded by the use of rods, and an effort was made to cushion the railbreaking impact of their unsprung weight by the use of steam springs. But George Stephenson was not by any means wholly employed in developing locomotives. He still had his other responsibilities as the Grand Allies' chief engineer, in charge of all machinery, and it was during this period, in 1815–16, that he invented his miners' safety lamp. Even in the railway sphere, he largely dealt with other matters. In partnership between 1815 and 1821 with William Losh he produced the best form of cast iron rail and other items of railway equipment, and he surveyed and built new railways as well, notably that at Hetton. This was opened in 1822; it was an eight-mile line, rising fron Hetton colliery to a 330 ft summit before falling to the Tyne, and had six stationary engines for haulage as well as five braked inclines on the download side and two locomotives to work on the level ground near Hetton.

Locomotives also worked two sections nearer the Tyne at first, but by 1826 had been laid aside and replaced by cable haulage. The Hetton railway was a model of its kind and the finest in England at the time of its opening, not least from the use of loading machines on the coal staithes at Wallsend, which lifted the whole wagon, contents and all, down into the hold of the ship.

George Stephenson by 1830 had built in fact only sixteen locomotives; a figure which includes the first four or five for the Stockton & Darlington line. Most of them served a decent term; one at Hetton remained in service until 1908, although much rebuilt; in her final form, although still of basic Stephenson outline with cylinders mounted vertically on the axis of the boiler, she had modern wheels and smokebox, and the boiler had clearly been renewed, apparently with a more or less conventional marine-type firebox and tubes. By 1828 the cost of locomotive haulage at Hetton had settled down to just under a farthing a ton-mile, for fuel and repairs; during October of that year an average of 1759 tons per day were shifted 1½ miles at a cost of £2 9*s* 2*d*, while horse haulage would have cost approximately £6 for equal work. But this was some years later, and the picture in the early 1820s was much more arguable.

The Killingworth and Hetton lines during the early 1820s were objects of considerable interest to a number of visitors who had thoughts of building railways in their own parts of the world, at home and abroad. Naturally they wanted to consider whether they ought to use locomotives; but the answer was not always easy. Let us take the case, for example, of the Stratford & Moreton Railway, a sixteen-mile line from Stratford-on-Avon to Moreton-in-the-Marsh, with a short branch to Shipston-on-Stour, which obtained its Act in 1821 and was opened five years later. Its main protagonist, William James, was a strong supporter of the locomotive, and had in mind that the S & M would become the first link in a chain of railways from Birmingham to London and Southampton (which explains perhaps why he should wish to build the line through a wholly rural area linking a town of only 1000 souls to the struggling canal at Stratford). He therefore proposed to the directors of the company in 1821 that the railway be built for locomotives, arguing that the additional cost of works to take their weight would be small and the saving in haulage cost would be considerable, even though the line included some quite heavy gradients. In 1822 George Stephenson wrote to him, giving details of loads and speeds obtainable on various inclinations, based on experience at Killingworth.

> The following is calculated for a load of 12 loaded waggons, each containing 3 tons, the waggons weighing 20–25 cwt [i.e. a trailing load of say 50 tons].
>
> Level: 4–8 mph
> $\frac{1}{16}$ in ascent per yard [1 in 576] $3\frac{1}{2}$–6 mph
> $\frac{2}{16}$ in ascent per yard [1 in 288] 3–5 mph
> $\frac{3}{16}$ in ascent per yard [1 in 192] 3–4 mph
> $\frac{1}{4}$ in ascent per yard [1 in 144] $2\frac{1}{2}$–3 mph
> $\frac{1}{16}$ in descent per yard 5–9 mph
> $\frac{2}{16}$ in descent per yard 6–10 mph
> $\frac{3}{16}$ in descent per yard 6–10 mph
> $\frac{1}{4}$ in descent per yard 6–10 mph
>
> I would not recommend my locomotive engine to travel on a line that ascends or descends more than $\frac{3}{16}$ in [1 in 192] where there is a load both ways, but if the load was always passing on a descending line the engines would return with the empty waggons up an ascent of 2 in per yard (1 in 72) or in a short distance from $\frac{5}{8}$ to $\frac{6}{8}$ ascent per yard [1 in 57 to 1 in 48]. The above is within the limits at which my Engines will work, but it is my wish to state it below its powers.

Partly because their line contained grades much steeper than 1 in 192 with a two-way traffic, but no doubt also because they were more conscious of the financial restrictions within which they had to work, the directors of the S & M were not convinced by James. One of them, John Greaves, produced a paper (quoted in an article by J. Simmons in the *Journal of Transport History*, May 1956), arguing that they should not use locomotives. His reasons, some of which were better than others, were:

1. The additional cost of forming bridges and track to carry the extra weight.
2. The superior resistance to oxidation of cast iron as opposed to wrought-iron rails, the latter being desirable for locomotives. (This argument seemed valid then, when wrought-iron rails had only recently been produced for the first time; it took some years of actual experience, and a published examination by Wood of the

wear and corrosion of early wrought-iron rails on the Tindale Fell railway, before doubts on this score were set at rest.)

3. The greater cost of track maintenance with the heavier axleload.
4. 'As it depends on the resistance offered by the iron rails to the surface of the wheels, for the application of power to the purposes of locomotion, it is necessary to create as much friction as possible at the contaction of the wheels with the plates, consequently the friction thus occasioned, together with the movement of the engine itself and the intendant carriage with coals and water for its supply, causes an extravagant waste of power, so that it may be justly questioned (when we bring into account all the expenses) whether a saving will be gained compared with horse-labour.' (Sixteen years later Nicholas Wood was still driven to complain how little the nature of friction was understood.)
5. 'The locomotive engines will not move a load when there is snow on the rails or in very wet weather.'
6. The frightening appearance of locomotives in action.
7. The danger of explosions.

This, in a nutshell, presented the anti-locomotive case of its time, omitting only the argument sometimes put forward based on the noxious fumes of coal smoke, allegedly so much more poisonous when burnt in motion. It shows what supporters of the locomotive had at that time to contend with; and remember that Greaves was the director of a railway company, so that he would not use the many arguments which were urged against the mere construction of a line itself. Yet, though technically wrong (or perhaps it is better to say shortsighted, since there was some merit in every one of his arguments except the fourth), Greaves was commercially, in that context, right. In fact locomotives were never used by that company, which depended entirely on horses; their second Act, in 1825, prohibited locomotives on that section of the line which for some miles out of Stratford ran beside the Oxford turnpike. The railway itself remained unprosperous.

The sad tale of the Stratford & Moreton makes an interesting contrast with the much better known success story of its exact contemporary, the Stockton & Darlington. This link between the coalfields of Bishop Auckland and the sea at Stockton, passing by way of Darlington, was a project over twenty-five miles in length. It had first been proposed as a canal, then as a railway surveyed by the South Wales tramroad engineer George Overton; however, in 1821, soon after the S & D Company succeeded in obtaining its Act, its main supporter, Edward Pease of Darlington, offered the task of building the line to George Stephenson. From that time on there never seems to have been any doubt that locomotives would be used on the line, although at the western end it was to be carried over two hills by two pairs of engine-powered inclines, and the remainder was all to be laid out for horses as well. Pease became a large shareholder when the firm of Robert Stephenson & Co. was founded as locomotive builders in 1823. The fact that the 1821 Act did not permit the Company to use locomotives was not regarded as important; it was necessary to obtain another Act anyhow to authorize certain of the diversions which Stephenson had made from Overton's route, and a suitable clause was duly inserted in that.

The essential difference between the two railways was that, although James had dreams of the S & M becoming a major artery of commerce, in fact it was a small and struggling rural outfit and never had, or even really believed it was likely to have, much business; while the S & D had firmly in its grasp right at the start a lucrative traffic. On Stephenson's commencement, Pease told him: 'In making the survey it must be borne in mind that this is for a great public way and to remain as long as any coal in the district remains.' With this attitude, the directors were not going to start cheeseparing; and if they decided to back the locomotive, they would back it firmly enough to make sure of success.

The S & D's first engine, *Locomotion*, was delivered to the railway shortly before its formal opening, on 27 September 1825, when she hauled a memorable trainload of coal and several hundred passengers, some invited and some not, from Shildon to Stockton. This was the world's first public steam-hauled train on any public railway. But for some years the Stockton & Darlington line was worked by both steam and horse power at the same time; the company was not staking everything on the economic success of the locomotive, and it was some time before this was clearly demonstrated. Horse traction in fact continued to be employed until as late as 1856, although after 1833 all the coal traffic was normally handled by steam and only passengers were dealt with, finally only on Sundays, by animal power.

Since the Stockton & Darlington provided a critical battlefield on which the locomotive proved itself, it is worth looking at the line in some detail. As opened in 1825, it commenced at Witton Park colliery, in the Wear Valley some two miles west of Bishop Auckland. Almost at once it crossed a ridge of hills into the Gaunless valley, climbing up the Etherley West incline and descending the Etherley East. Just over a mile of level horseworked track then ran across the Gaunless to the foot of Brusselton West Bank, where another pair of inclines, Brusselton West and East, carried the line across Brusselton Hill and down to New Shildon. At Etherley Bank Top and at Brusselton Bank Top were engine houses, where fixed steam engines (also built by Robert Stephenson & Co.) drew loads up the hill. They were both rather unusual inclines. The 30 hp engine at Etherley was needed to power Etherley West, since here the grade was against the load, but it was assisted by empty wagons descending at the same time on the other track. Etherley East, on the other hand, was a conventional self-acting gravity-powered incline, engine assistance not being needed. Brusselton, which had a 60 hp engine, was arranged otherwise. There were two winding drums of different diameters coupled together on the same shaft at Brusselton Bank Top, so that one loaded train descending the shorter Brusselton East Bank (Shildon being at a higher level that the Gaunless) helped the engine draw the next up the longer West Bank. Both inclines were single track without a midway passing loop; and in order to return the rope it was necessary that successive pairs of trains should always cross the ridge in alternating directions.

The more one stops and thinks about this the more complicated it gets, and certainly according to the records operation of these inclines caused a number of serious headaches in the early years, with ropes becoming wrongly wound on the drum and all kinds of other problems. But little has been written about exactly how the Brusselton inclines were worked in practice, and we have to piece the method together. Passing the trains at the summit would present no difficulty; all that was needed was a simple loop on a level section, where a train in one direction could wait while the incline was running through the opposite cycle in the other direction. But working the rope must have been complex. The winding drum was situated above the track, and so a train arriving at the summit, with the rope attached to the leading wagon, could not have been drawn forward far enough for the other rope to be attached to the last wagon for the descent. Nor would it have been able to roll forward into the required position by gravity, because if there was such a gradient on the summit loop it would have prevented any corresponding movement by a train going the other way; and although it would have been possible in theory to arrange that the two tracks of the summit passing loop were graded in opposite directions the evidence of a painting of Brusselton Bank Top lying derelict after the inclines were replaced by a tunnel during the 1850s indicates that this was not done, as the tracks were side by side. Probably horses were used to position trains suitably, although the evidence of letters passing between Robert Stephenson and Timothy Hackworth, quoted in Young's biography of the latter, speaking of arms which carried the rope off and onto the drum, and of troubles with the rope bunching, then giving off slack and causing runaways, indicates that alternative methods were at any rate tried.

One piece of evidence, from Rastrick's account of the railway in 1829, also casts an indirect light on the method of working at Brusselton. He said that the engine had sufficient power to draw up twelve loaded wagons weighing some 40 tons, and often did so without waiting for a balancing load. This implies that, in order to return the rope to the foot of the other incline, a match wagon of some kind must have been used; and if special incline wagons were indeed used, then it would have been possible to fit them with an arm holding the rope clear of any part of the ordinary wagons and so the rope could have been attached to the downhill or to the uphill end of trains. This would ease the positioning problem at the summit. One edition of Wood's *Treatise* devotes an entire engraved plate to diagrams of possible permutations of rope workings.

Brusselton East Bank ended at New Shildon, where the company's first locomotive works and depot were situated; for the remaining distance of some twenty-two miles to Stockton via Darlington (North Road) the railway was single track, with passing loops able to take two horse-drawn trains at a time (a horse pulling anything up to six wagons) every half-mile or so. It was only on this section that locomotives were used. The line fell gradually on a more or less continual gradient to the quays at Stockton, Shildon being nearly 450 feet above sea level. The average inclination was between 1 in 200 and 1 in 250, quite steep enough to be a very great help to the locomotives dealing with the preponderantly downhill traffic.

Four locomotives of Killingworth type were built by Robert Stephenson & Co and delivered to the S & D in 1825–26: no. 1 *Locomotion*, no. 2 *Hope*, no. 3 *Black Diamond*, and no. 4 *Diligence*. All were basically similar, with a boiler with single flue two feet in diameter. The fire was contained at one end of the flue by means of a firebrick wall in the middle, and the flue was carried out of the far end of the boiler and turned upwards to form the chimney. All four engines had vertical cylinders mounted centrally in the boiler and above each axle. The bulk of the traffic was at first handled by horses, while the locomotive experiment was pursued in cooperation by George Stephenson (in control of the firm of builders at Newcastle during his son Robert's absence abroad from 1824 to 1827), and Timothy Hackworth, the man on the spot at Shildon.

They had their troubles. Perhaps the mildest was poor steaming. There had been no precedent for working locomotives over such long distances; on the much shorter Tyneside colliery railways there was a good chance to complete the run before the steam and water in the boiler at the start had been seriously depleted. But on a 22-mile run water had to be converted into steam, and the boiler replenished with cold water as well, at the rate at which it was required by the cylinders. There was little that could be done to improve the steam-raising capacity of these boilers as they stood except to increase the draught caused by the blast: Stephenson's practice had been to arrange the exhaust nozzles in the chimney so that they created very little blast, since on short runs it was not required and fire throwing could thus be avoided. But Stephenson certainly knew about the draught-creating effect of the blast, as indeed Trevithick had found before him after a few days' trials at Penydaren. Hackworth altered the S & D engines so that the exhaust did create a draughting effect, with three consequences: (*a*) the engines then steamed adequately; (*b*) considerable quantities of fire were thrown, with the result that in dry weather the company had to station beaters along the lineside to extinguish conflagrations and avoid damage to crops and woodlands; and (*c*) Timothy Hackworth's partisans, led by his son John, in after years attempted to prove that Hackworth had invented the blast, as everything else of merit in locomotives, and that the contribution of the Stephensons was greatly overstated, as indeed it had been, notably by Samuel Smiles. This then became a very dreary and acrimonious argument, an early example of the dispute of precedence between designer and executant for the award of credit for new inventions. The author declares his preference: in principle, credit for a new idea should go to the man who first thinks of it.

Two other problems were more serious. One was boiler explosions. Both *Locomotion* and *Hope* exploded during 1828, killing their drivers. Probably in each case only the flue collapsed, since both engines were rebuilt and continued in service for a number of years afterwards; but even so that was bad enough. Probably the reason for the explosion was decided to be the engine crew tampering with the safety valve, which in the original form was held down simply by a weighted lever, all too easy to weight a bit more; at any rate Hackworth designed and fitted a new type of lock-up safety valve fitted with a set of plate springs set in a frame, much more difficult to interfere with; but possibly the reason could also have been low water uncovering the top of the fire flue and leading to overheating and failure. There was no such thing then as a water gauge on any boiler, and the crew had to judge the level by means of two or three testcocks, trying whether steam or water came out of them when opened. Since even at a pressure of only 50 lb per square inch water in a boiler is hot enough to flash instantly into steam on being released to the atmosphere the only way to judge whether steam or water is coming out is to listen to the noise on opening the cock (water sounding at a rather lower pitch) and it is not always easy to avoid a mistake which could be a fatal one. It seems, incidentally, that the water gauge glass is due to John Rastrick, since the first record of one on any locomotive appears in an account of four built by Foster and Rastrick of Stourbridge in 1829.

The third main problem, not quite so dramatic but just as deadly to the locomotive's chances, was the complex situation resulting from the lack of springing and the use of cast iron wheels. Stephenson's steam springs had fallen out of favour by the mid-1820s, and by 1827 were no longer in use anywhere. Whether or not the S&D engines had them when delivered is uncertain, but probably they were unsprung, with nothing more than a three-point suspension (having one axle carried on a single central bearing) to accommodate them to the unevennesses of the road. It is not clear that they all had even this; certainly *Locomotion* in its present state is quite unsprung and with all four bearings solidly mounted on the frames. Why the steam spring had been discarded is also uncertain, though it must have presented maintenance difficulties and been only partly useful as a spring. Theoretically it is unsound to have any springing on an axle driven directly from a cylinder mounted above it, since any movement of the axle on the springs brings about a corresponding shift in the motion of the piston in the cylinder. In practice this can be accommodated by allowing plenty of room between the piston at the end of its stroke and the end of the cylinder; heavy impacts on a cast iron cylinder end set inside a boiler were things to be avoided at all costs. But this is an unsatisfactory answer, since it leads to having a relatively large proportion of the cylinder unswept by the piston. This 'clearance volume' still has to be filled with steam and waste results. Probably the abandonment of steam springs was due to a realization of this point combined with all their practical difficulties.

However, locomotive wheels were still solid iron castings, because at that time there was no other way of making an all-metal wheel; and experience soon showed that they were simply not capable of standing up to the strains and stresses of the hammering they got from carrying these quite large unsprung weights. (A Stephenson locomotive in working order with tender is quoted as weighing ten tons, but this contemporary record may be a bit of an understatement; *Locomotion* when put in steam for the 1925 S & D centenary was put on the scales without her tender and found to weigh 8 tons 8 cwt.) Hackworth also faced the difficulty that there was no lathe at Shildon works big enough to turn the 4 ft diameter engine wheels. His answer to this was ingenious, and one that he adopted permanently: he designed a wheel formed by two separate castings. The inner one was set on the axle and turned true in the lathe; the outer one was then set on the inner, and trued up and fastened by means of wooden plugs and iron wedges. Since both castings were extremely strong and the wedged joint gave a certain amount of resilience, these wheels were successful. They were also fitted with unflanged wrought-iron tyres or 'rims'. Hackworth standardized on this type of wheel until the mid 1840s.

The development of satisfactory steel springs was tackled by Nicholas Wood, and Hackworth did not at first follow him. Between 1825 and 1828 Wood developed a laminated plate spring and fitted it to the Stephenson locomotives at Killingworth; these were the first locomotives to be properly sprung. Although in theory open to the same objection arising out of excessive clearance volume as the steam springs, in practice the movement of a plate spring is only restricted and therefore the cylinder problem was not so acute. However, the use of springs on locomotives with vertical cylinders remained uncommon.

Despite these difficulties and the expense that resulted from them, the Stockton and Darlington soon decided that locomotives were worth persevering with. The subsequent locomotive history of the line will be studied in the next chapter, as it is of considerable interest; it is sufficient to record here that as early as 1827, before any other machines had been delivered, the directors claimed in a report to the company's shareholders that locomotives showed an overall saving of 30 per cent compared with the cost of horse haulage. Whatever special unstated allowances they may have been making for development costs, this at least shows that they had faith in them.

An interesting account of railway development in England and Wales in 1826–27 is provided by a report made by the German engineers Carl von Oeynhausen and Heinrich von Dechen, who toured the country that winter. They give an account of three locomotive-worked railways: the S&D, the Hetton, and the Middleton. It is interesting to note that while the S&D machines, with a favourable grade, were at that time handling trains of up to twenty wagons totalling about 75 tons, the older engines on the Middleton were hauling between twenty-six and thirty-two wagons, weighing 100 tons or more. Blenkinsop did not yet have cause to consider the rack rail a mistake!

Among the non-locomotive worked railways they visited was the Plymouth & Dartmoor, a 25¾-mile line opened for the most part in 1823, worked by horses and rising from Sutton Pool on Plymouth Harbour to Princetown on a fairly steady climb at about 1 in 100. (Part of the course was later used by the Princetown branch of the GWR, now also closed.) Commercially this line was perhaps as inexplicable as the Stratford and Moreton, but it was very well equipped; the visitors were astonished to find that it possessed a lathe big enough to turn its wagon wheels accurately on their axles, the implication being that other railways were generally content with rough castings more or less circular. It also possessed a 4-ton mobile crane for loading granite blocks; the only other similar vehicle they saw mounted on rails was in a quarry near Whitehaven.

The plateways they visited in South Wales failed to impress them; most were dilapidated and evidently considerable trouble was caused by dirt on the rails. A horse could seldom pull more than a 2-ton load, and in an endeavour to reduce the nuisance by cutting through the dirt on the plates wheels had been tapered down to very narrow treads, sometimes as little as $\frac{1}{8}$ inch across, which led to great wear of both wheels and rails.

During the 1820s the promoters of the slowly growing number of railway schemes had three basically different methods of operation to choose from. The earlier problem—edge or plate rail?—had been pretty decisively settled by experience in favour of the former by about 1810, and few if any new tramroads were laid down after that date. The choice now was whether to stay faithful to the horse, or to adopt steam power; and if so, whether to use locomotives or fixed engines. Technology had not a great deal to offer in aid of Dobbin, although it did have something; where the line could be so arranged that there was a long moderate gradient favouring the load, trains could run down by gravity taking the horse with them, and he need only exert himself to haul the empties back uphill again. The Stockton & Darlington was such a line, though the falling grade was not sufficiently constant to allow a continuous gravity run all the way; nevertheless, a 'dandy-cart' was provided at the rear of each train, and on reaching the top of a sufficiently steep grade the horse would be unhitched from the traces, and without further ado he would make his own way to the dandy car and jump in it as it rumbled past him. The sight of these heavy cart-horses knowing exactly what to do, and leaping nimbly into a moving vehicle from behind, became quite a well-known attraction to the district.

Fixed engines had been used to haul trains for some time before the S & D was opened; Wood states that the first was installed by S. Cooke in 1808 to carry the railway from Urpeth colliery up Birtley Fell, between Durham and Newcastle. But in the years after the rather rudimentary efforts at Brusselton and Etherley the system was considerably developed, at least on paper, in an effort to show how long main line railways could be worked on this principle. Fixed engines could be used in two ways: to draw trains up and down inclines, or to draw them along the level.

Inclines were the simpler proposition. However steep the grade, no additional difficulty of principle presented itself, although clearly a safety factor had to be taken into account and few rope-worked inclines at this time were steeper than about 1 in 8. The limiting factor was more the other way; what was the easiest grade down which a descending train would drag the rope? Wood examined this question in his *Treatise on Railroads*, and came to the conclusion based on experience of inclines in operation in the Newcastle district that 1 in 50 was not steep enough to allow reliable operation in all states of weather. He gave his opinion that 1 in 37 was the gentlest practicable grade, and that on inclines not much longer than 715 yards, or say half a mile at most. Length was important because although the friction due to the drum and the bending of the rope was more or less constant, that due to the rollers carrying it between the rails was not. Whether or not an incline was powered or assisted by an engine did not materially affect the issue, since enough steam could always be put on to overcome the resistance caused by the engine. Self-acting inclines, on the other hand, needed to be considerably steeper, since the descending loads also had to drag up the ascending empties; commonly they were at least as steep as 1 in 20.

Where the descending grade was insufficiently steep, or where there was no descent at all, haulage by fixed engines involved the use of an endless rope, moving in a circular path, to which trains in each direction could be attached. There was one obvious difficulty about this which precluded the use of the system at first; the rope would stretch, and so by losing its grip on the winding drum become useless. However, this was dealt with during the late 1820s by devising a compensating system in which the rope passed through a pair of multiple-sheaved pulleys, on one of which was hung a heavy weight which could move up and down in a pit; in this way slack could continually be taken up and released and a constant tension maintained. There was an alternative to the endless rope, by which one fixed engine would drag along a train which had tied on behind it the idle returning rope being paid out from an adjacent engine; but although Wood describes such a system it is uncertain whether one was ever in fact built.

The endless cable became a perfectly satisfactory system from the operating point of view. There is was, endlessly moving; all one needed to do was attach a train to it. There were a number of possible variations on the idea. In its simplest form, it could be applied to a straightforward double-track railway, with the rope moving outwards on one track and returning on the other. It need never stop, so long as means of coupling and uncoupling trains to it while it was in motion could be devised, and in this case there was no need to arrange any balance between trains moving in opposite directions. Otherwise, it could also be applied to a single-line railway, with passing loops at the winding engines and possibly in between. In this case it would not be possible to arrange for non-stop working, and to ensure that trains met at the intermediate passing place it would be necessary to operate on the same principle as an incline, with 'up' and 'down' trains attached to the rope at each terminus while it was stationary, the winding engine being started on a given signal. (How to give this signal was something of a problem in the days before the telegraph, wherever the termini were out of sight, but the usual answer was to provide either, as on the Cromford & High Peak, a light message-cable to ring a bell or work a pointer, or, as at Camden and Euston, a pneumatic tube blowing a whistle.)

Over the years cable operation of moderately graded lines has been carried out often enough to prove its practicability. The only conventional public railways in Britain to use the system throughout were the Durham & Sunderland and London & Blackwall, which applied it during the 1840s for a number of years quite successfully in its double-track form, even though by that time the sight of passenger and goods trains trundling along without a concomitant column of steam, but instead with a continual squeaking and groaning of the sheaves and rollers like the gibbering of noonday ghosts, had become an anachronistic peculiarity. Cable haulage was at one time widely used by street tramways, and still survives on the two famous San Francisco cable car lines, while a number of underground railways (notably the Glasgow subway) also used it for many years. Nor was incline operation using a non-continuous rope something so inherently unreliable and subject to interruption that it had to be confined to industrial and colliery lines; several grades on locomotive-worked main-line railways used fixed engines for many years, usually in combination with locomotive power. One thinks of the 1 in 27 at Oldham on the Lancashire & Yorkshire, and the 1 in 75 grade out of Euston on the London & Birmingham, where for a number of years the winding engines assisted the train, engine and all, until more powerful locomotives were able to make the climb on their own; or the rather similar Cowlairs incline of 1 in 42 out of Glasgow (Queen Street), where cable working survived into the twentieth century. Here an ascending train was assisted partly by the winding engine and partly by a balancing tank engine, coupled to the descending rope, steaming downgrade usually rather harder than the ascending main-line engine. In all these cases a form of slip shackle was used so that there was no need to stop at the summit to detach from the cable.

The weakness of the principle of haulage by fixed engines was not so much its awkwardness, which was not insuperable, but its cost. The trouble was that engines had to be built, manned, and kept in operation approximately every half-mile. Because the failure of one could cause an interruption of traffic throughout the line, which might be tolerable on a colliery railway but could not be permitted to happen on a public main line of any importance, provision had to be made that the cable on each section might be driven from either end, which meant in turn that the sections had to be shorter than they might otherwise have been and rather more reserve capacity had to be provided in every engine. It all added up.

There was a considerable amount of discussion during the late 1820s as to whether the Liverpool & Manchester Railway, the world's first important public intercity main line, then under construction, should adopt locomotive or fixed engine haulage. Certainly a lot of heat was developed; the company had an enormous board with over thirty directors, and it is a well-known principle of business that the amount of discussion required before coming to a decision increases more than proportionately with the number of people desirous of joining the discussion. The Stephenson party, as partisans of the locomotive, had a field day, and a degree of passion was lent to their argument by their knowledge of the embranglements they had got themselves into at Brusselton. The company had commissioned James Walker and John Rastrick, as independent engineer advisers, during 1828 to study the alternatives and report them; and their recommendation was in favour of fixed engines. The report was savaged. Nicholas Wood wrote, not with absolute justification, of the problems involved in the operation; which track would be free, which rope disengaged, and so on, with a double scissors crossover required at every engine: 'The inconvenience, delay, and risk attending the carriages thus passing from one line to the other, and travelling in different directions upon different parts of the same line of road, confine the use of this mode of transit exclusively to private lines: upon public lines it would produce inexplicable, and irremediable, confusion.' Timothy Hackworth's well-known remark in a letter of encouragement to Robert Stephenson in 1829, written within a mile of Brusselton, is worth quoting again: 'Do not discompose yourself, my dear sir: if you express your manly, firm, and decided opinion, you have done your part as their adviser. And if it happens to be read some day in the newspapers "Whereas the Liverpool and Manchester Railway has been strangled by ropes", we shall not accuse you of guilt in being accessory either before or after the fact.'

But really the matter was onesided. Walker and Rastrick were only barely in favour of fixed engines, and their argument was more or less 'well, a line like this ought to be able to afford them'. Their only solid reason for preferring cable haulage was fear of boiler explosion. It is interesting to note that they made a similar report at about the same time to the directors of the Leeds & Selby Railway, but decided there in favour of locomotives on the grounds that on this less important line there would not be sufficient traffic to justify the extra cost of fixed engines. They were not in any way challenging whether locomotives could do the job, even on the Liverpool & Manchester. The alternative before the L & M Board was therefore a simple one. If fixed engines were adopted, fifty-four would need to be installed along the thirty miles of line, and together with their fittings and the cost of the rope, etc., would require a capital outlay of £81,000. To work the estimated amount of traffic, forty-eight locomotive engines would be required, at a total capital outlay of £28,000. Walker and Rastrick estimated a 25 per cent economy in operating costs in favour of fixed engines, but their figures were disputed; certainly although the experience of Hetton colliery agreed with their estimate, the Stockton & Darlington provided figures of their 1826 operating costs per ton-mile as 23/25ths of a farthing for locomotives, and $1\frac{3}{16}$ and $1\frac{3}{8}$ pence respectively for Etherley and Brusselton (admittedly not a fair comparison because of the gradients, let alone the other difficulties, but the fact that balanced workings up and down hill did not equate to the same thing as level track was not then widely appreciated). It was therefore felt unsafe to rely on any operating cost figures either way, especially as all admitted that locomotives were much more capable than fixed engines of improvement.

But the clincher was that once any money was spent on fixed engines the company was committed to spend the whole of it; one engine was pointless, it was fifty-four or nothing, and not much of a return if they later changed their minds. But fixed engines could always, if necessary, be installed later. Locomotives could be experimented with very cheaply in an endeavour to find out more certainly if they could meet the railway's needs; one locomotive or a very few would be sufficient for this purpose; and even if all forty-eight were built and some years later the directors were to change their minds and abandon them, the loss would still be much smaller. Really, there was only one possible decision for the directors to take, and they took it. The plans for fixed engines went into the pigeonhole, and on 20 April 1829 the Board resolved to offer a prize of £500 for the best locomotive conforming to certain conditions as to weight and performance, the winner to be determined as the result of a competitive trial to be held the following October on a completed stretch of the railway at Rainhill. By this momentous if inevitable decision the future of the locomotive was put to the test.

CHAPTER FOUR

Locomotive Development, 1825-1834

The first four Stockton & Darlington locomotives were, as we have seen, all basically of Stephenson's Killingworth type; and we have seen how they fared, and to what extent they were modified and improved by Hackworth. In spite of the two boiler explosions already mentioned, they lasted quite well; *Locomotion* herself remained in service till 1841, latterly on branch line work, and from 1841 to 1847 did a further spell of duty as a colliery pumping engine. In 1850 as part of the anniversary celebrations she was mounted on a pedestal in front of Darlington (North Road) station, and moved to her present position on the platforms at Darlington main station some years later, emerging to run again under her own steam for the further celebrations in 1925. The other three engines were withdrawn during the 1840s and scrapped. We have the authority of Robert Metcalf, at one time the foreman of a contractor's gang building the line and later an engineman, given in a letter to Edward Pease written in 1856, that *Locomotion* is still as she was.

> When no. 1 Engine was put to yon Mount afront the station there was a great deal discushion abo̓ut her I could condicked them in many words but I thought it was not my place to do so she all in original state excepting the tender it was a water barrel put on to top on an end on a muck waggon and she travled as nigh as I can tell for two years before she got a proper tender.

These engines gave sufficiently encouraging results for the locomotive experiment to be continued, and the Company started to look round for some more. The question at first was, who was to build them? Robert Stephenson & Co were working under difficulties, as Robert had gone abroad in June 1824 as engineer to a speculative mining enterprise in Columbia, not returning until November 1827. Since George Stephenson could not devote much

1 A wagon used in the early 19th century on a plateway in Cornwall, now preserved at Camborne, with its original drawgear

2 A Tyneside wagonway of the time of the first locomotives; a view of the Church Pit, Wallsend. The wagon in the centre stands at the head of an incline with cable haulage

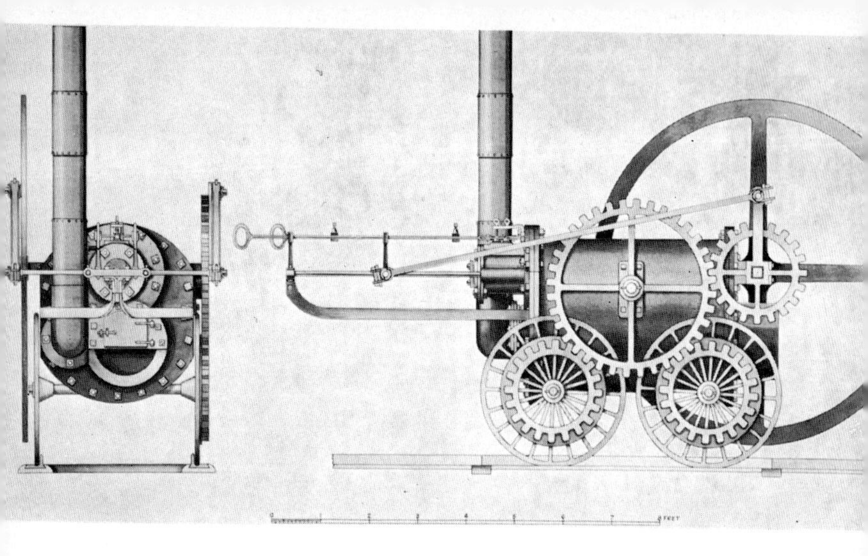

3 A reconstructed drawing of Trevithick's Penydaren engine

4 Hedley's Wylam locomotive, as running in 1825 on eight wheels

(*Above*) Robert Stephenson's 'America' of 1828, similar to the 'Lancashire itch' except for valvegear. 6 (*Below*) Stephenson's 'Locomotion'

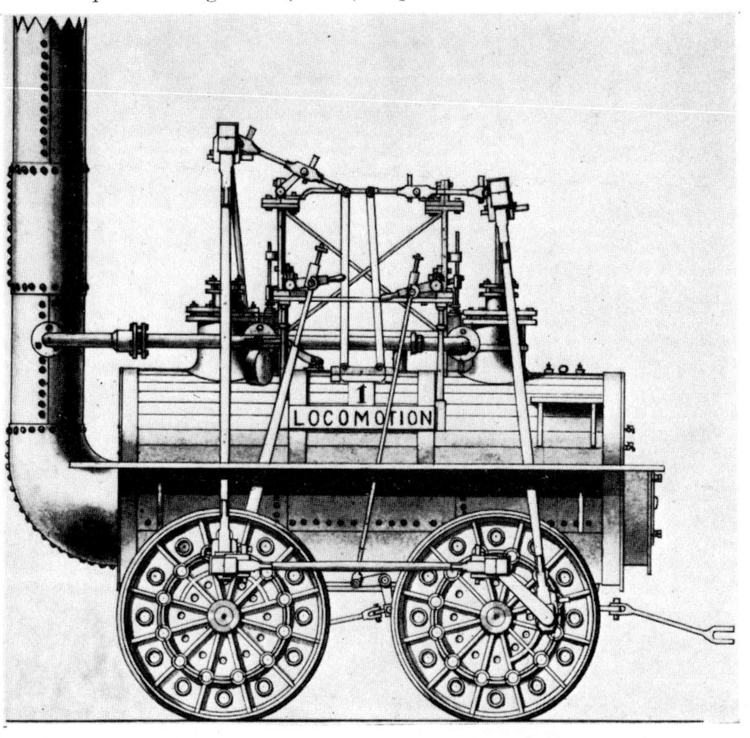

7 Hackworth's 'Royal George', as completed for the Stockton and Darlington in 1827

8 Galloway's 'Caledonian' running on the Liverpool and Manchester in 183
coupled to a typical first-class coach. This machine adopted Hackworth's idea
a dummy crankshaft, but placed centrally between the wheels

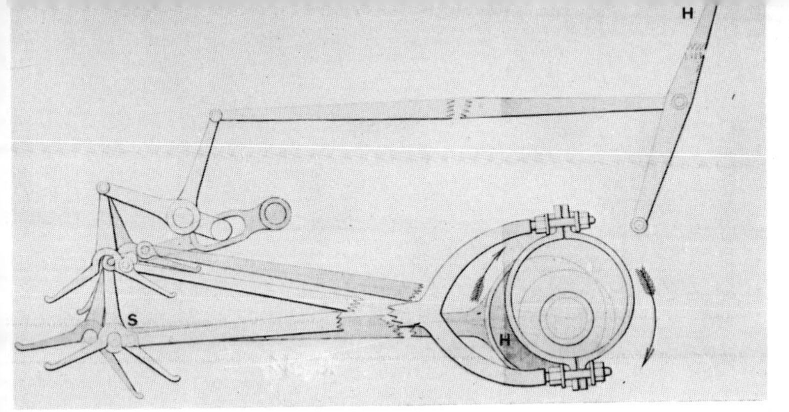

'orrester's arrangement of the gab gear using two eccentrics per cylinder (1834); means of the reversing lever (H) the driver could lower one gab onto the valve pin (at S) while raising the other gab clear. Wood's drawing rather confusingly ›ws both gabs in both possible positions

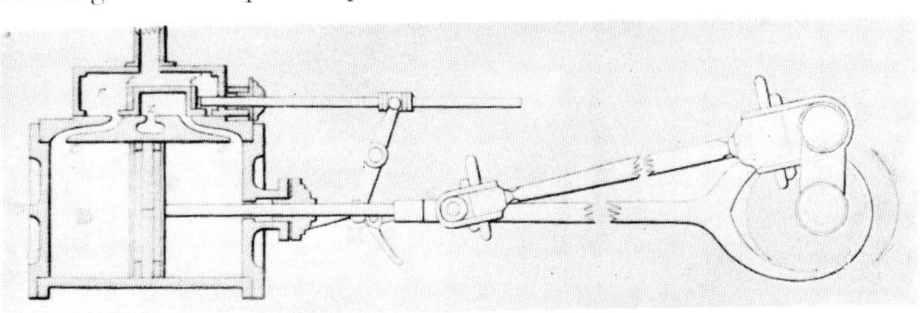

(Above) A diagram of cylinder and valve, and related parts, c. 1835. Steam ers the valve-chamber from the boiler at *r*, pressing the valve (*e-e*) onto its seat; exhaust is through the passage marked *z*. As shown, the piston is moving from to right, and the valve from right to left, shortly to close the admission and aust ports. 11 (*Below*) Two varieties of built-up wheel using bar spokes of eft) and L(*right*) shape, both cast into the nave

12 The remains of the Rainhill 'Rocket' at South Kensington, in front of Robert Stephenson's portrait

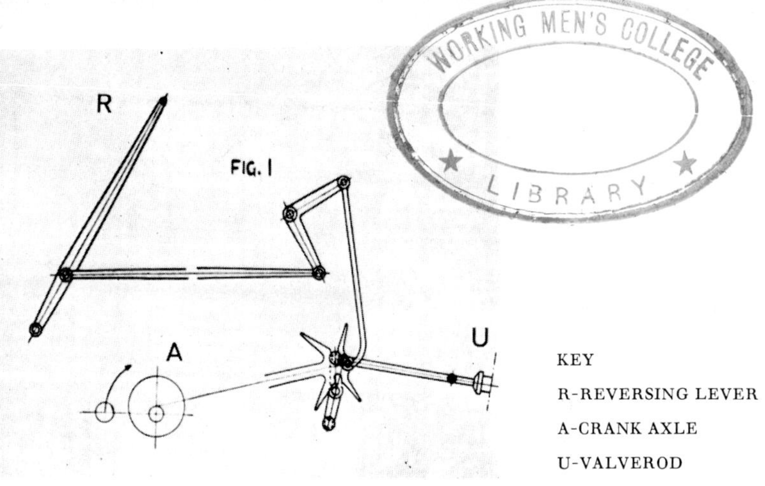

KEY

R-REVERSING LEVER

A-CRANK AXLE

U-VALVEROD

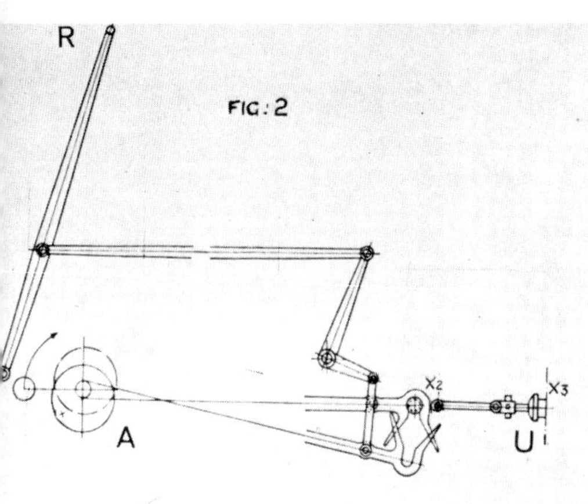

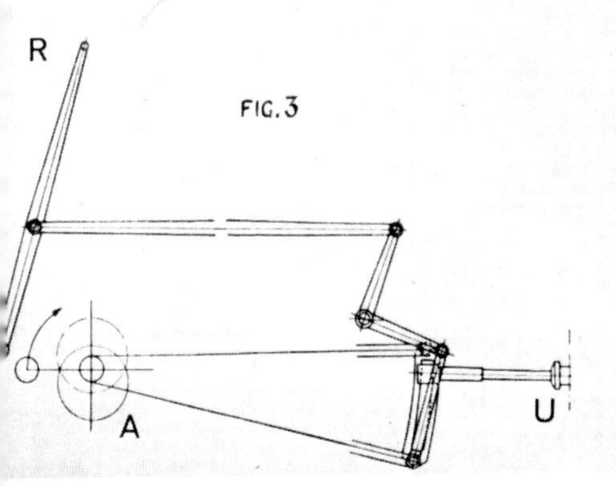

13 Three stages in the development of the Stephenson valve gear: (i) an 1835 arrangement with one eccentric per cylinder, with X-gab reversing by driving opposite ends of a rocking lever; (ii) a typical 1840 arrangement, with two eccentrics per cylinder and Y-gabs driving the valve alternately; (iii) the first form of Stephenson Link motion

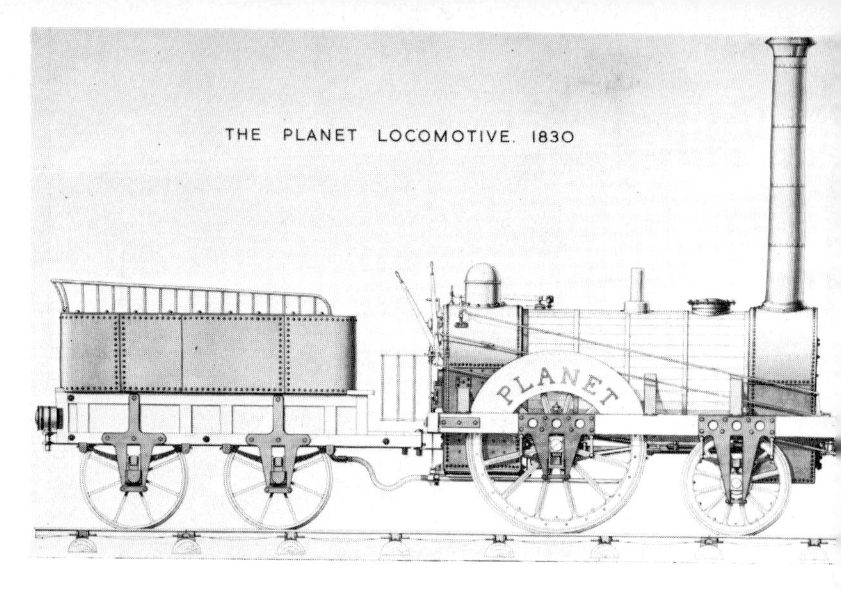

14 (*Above*) The prototype 'Planet', built for the Liverpool and Manchester in 1830; the first locomotive with horizontal cylinders mounted at the front
15 (*Below*) Bury's variation on the 'Planet' type, as built for the London and Birmingham, with D-shaped firegrate and bar frames

time to the business it was managed, in what little time he could spare from his ironworks at Bedlington near Morpeth, by Michael Longridge. Of the others who had built locomotives, Trevithick was also in Columbia and a broken man; Fenton, Murray and Wood declined to build any more 'until they become a regular article of commerce'; and the private works at Wylam were not particularly interested. In any case, Hackworth himself had been foreman smith at Wylam when Hedley's engines were built, so there was little knowhow there which was not available to the Stockton & Darlington.

Robert Wilson of Gateshead, however, offered to build a locomotive, which was tried on the line during 1826. It did not long survive, and there are no drawings or detailed descriptions of it, but it seems clear that it must have been a very interesting machine. It was four-wheeled, and powered by four cylinders, all presumably vertical, but probably mounted outside the boiler and driving directly downwards on to each wheel. In this way Wilson dispensed with coupling rods and, according to Zerah Colburn in his *Locomotive Engineering* (1864), this was the first engine in which a pair of wheels was worked directly by two pistons acting on cranks at right-angles to each other. (Trevithick's London engine had had direct drive, but only one cylinder.) Legend has it that it was because of the curious and doubtless rapid exhaust noise Wilson's engine made as it went along that the men christened it the *Chittaprat*. However, for one reason or another it was not a success; the company purchased it but laid it aside.

Two locomotives were built for the line in 1827. The first was the *Experiment*, built by Robert Stephenson & Co, which was not delivered to Shildon until January 1828 but which had been inspected by von Oeynhausen nearly a year previously. L. T. C. Rolt in his biography of the Stephensons suggests she may have been tried meanwhile on the Killingworth line, where George Stephenson and Nicholas Wood could keep an eye on her, which is likely enough. In building her, the elder Stephenson broke away from the vertical cylinder layout which he had used hitherto, and tried to find a more satisfactory disposition of the machinery. She had two cylinders, mounted horizontally together inside the boiler, and like the Penydaren engine driving out of one end of the barrel. But instead of gear wheels, each pistonrod drove on to the end of an arm connected to a shaft mounted in a bracket above the boiler; and at the outer end of each shaft there was another arm which drove, by means of a long connecting rod, the wheel at the opposite end of the machine. The boiler was still of the straight-flue type, but contained one remarkably advanced device intended to assist steaming. The firegrate was formed of water tubes, connecting with the boiler near the firedoor and at the chimney end leading into a cylindrical drum mounted in the front half of the main flue so that the hot gases could pass all round it, except where it was connected to the top of the flue and so back into the boiler by a rectangular casting. In effect, this formed a sort of thermic syphon, and although it was not repeated (as something better soon turned up) it seems to have worked satisfactorily. Part of the exhaust steam was also used to preheat the feedwater, the first time this had been done on a locomotive.

As delivered to Shildon the *Experiment* was four-wheeled, but in this form she proved too hard on the track and so she was rebuilt in a new frame with six wheels. At the same time the opportunity was taken to fit her throughout with plate springs (she may or may not have been fully sprung originally). Due to the rather prominent action of the arms and rods on the outside of the engine, the Shildon men nicknamed her 'Old Elbows'. Hackworth's biographer pours scorn on her, but he had an axe to grind; certainly the record shows that she gave useful service for a number of years, and improved upon earlier machines.

The other locomotive was Hackworth's rebuild of the *Chittaprat*, which was christened the *Royal George*. In this modified form it was certainly the most powerful and successful locomotive up to that date. She made use, according to the records, of the *Chittaprat*'s boiler, though Young says that this was enlarged both in length and in diameter, a statement which if true would be surprising; at any rate, it was definitely a considerably larger boiler, with a return flue which more than doubled the heating surface in comparison with *Locomotion*. Like the *Experiment*, she also had a feedwater heater. She had two cylinders, mounted as the *Chittaprat*'s probably were, externally at one end of the boiler and driving vertically downwards with a direct rod connection to the leading pair of wheels, which were unsprung. The other four wheels (since she was an 0–6–0) were coupled by rods and carried the weight through two large plate springs bearing across both axleboxes, one on either side. During

1828 this engine was claimed to show a saving of 53 per cent compared with the cost of horse working; and although it was said to have cost £425 to build it was sold out of service in 1840 for £550.

This was the prototype of the Hackworth pattern of locomotive, which it is worth considering now out of chronological sequence since although it formed an evolutionary blind alley it was not without interest. The distinguishing features of the design were: (1) the use of a return-flue boiler, with the chimney and firedoor next to each other at the same end of the boiler: and/or (2) cylinders mounted vertically at one end of the boiler. Where the return-flue boiler was used, two tenders were almost always provided; one at the chimney end to carry coal and provide a platform on which the fireman stood, the other at the cylinder end carrying water and also the driver. The success of the *Royal George* and of the similar *Victory* which followed in 1829 was really due to its combination of adequate boiler capacity and efficiency, with mechanical reliability brought about through simplicity. The economic performance which resulted was the justification for the development of Hackworth's design, despite its weaknesses.

The more serious weakness of the *Royal George* was the fact that the driving wheels were unsprung, for the reasons already explained. In the *Majestic* and *Wilberforce* classes of 1830, both 0–6–0s of generally similar dimensions to the *Royal George*, Hackworth achieved springing of all axles combined with minimal cylinder clearance volume by mounting the cylinders (still vertical) beyond the wheelbase so that they drove a dummy crankshaft, from which the drive was transmitted horizontally to the wheels by rods. The *Majestic* class were fitted with a modified single-flue boiler in which the last four feet of flue were replaced by multiple tubes; the cylinders were mounted on an overhanging framework ahead of the chimney smokebox. These engines needed only one tender. The *Wilberforce* class had a form of return-flue boiler which is of considerable interest as it improved on Trevithick's: the firetube led into a drum which was considerably larger in cross-section, occupying most of the water space. From the sections of this drum which overlapped the firetube, many small tubes were led back to a smokebox which encircled the firedoor. Thus the boiler was considerably more efficient, if more expensive to build, and offered the maintenance advantage of the later marine pattern boiler in that the entire

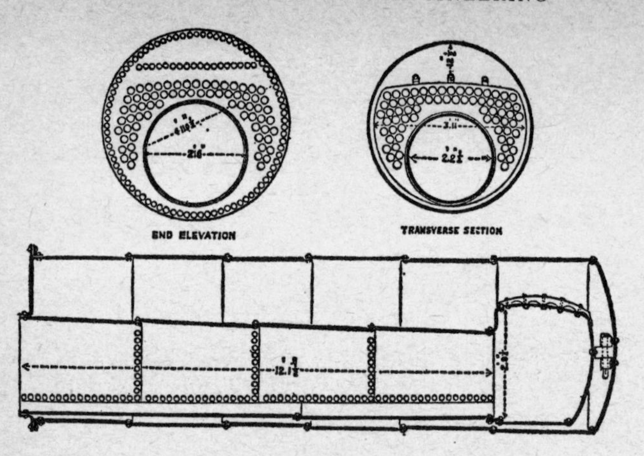

Figure 4 The final development of the Hackworth boiler, as fitted to the 'Wilberforce' class

fire and tube assembly could readily be withdrawn and replaced without any trouble from the complicated stayed surfaces needed with a firebox. The *Wilberforce* cylinders and dummy crankshaft were mounted on a frame ahead of the blind end of the boiler, and two separate tenders were needed as on the *Royal George*.

A number of locomotives were constructed to these patterns, chiefly for the Stockton and Darlington and other lines nearby, although three like the *Royal George* were built for Canada as late as 1838. They gave good service, so long as they were kept on low-speed freight work, but they still suffered from the other drawback of the vertical cylinder layout: the alternating up and down strokes of pistons on opposite sides of the engine made them very unsteady, and they were apt to roll about, especially when they had been put on springs. Placing the cylinders outside the wheelbase, as on the *Wilberforce* and *Majestics*, only made this worse. These engines churned away satisfactorily enough up and down the Stockton and Darlington, but even in 1840 the speed of coal trains on that line was very strictly limited to 6 mph, and drivers who were caught going faster were summarily fined or dismissed.

Hackworth's final pattern of locomotive, the *Leader* class of 1842, therefore dispensed with the vertical cylinders, and while retaining the *Wilberforce* pattern boiler mounted the cylinders at an angle of 30° at the opposite end to the chimney, driving directly on to the wheels by connecting rods. One of these engines, the *Derwent* of 1845, is preserved at Darlington station alongside *Locomotion*, but minus one tender. Following Hackworth's retirement some rather similar-looking engines were built by Thomas Bouch, but they had normal multitubular boilers and the cylinders (still steeply inclined) were mounted at the smokebox end, while two tenders were retained although no longer strictly necessary. With these, the Stockton and Darlington rejoined the main stream of locomotive development while making a final gesture of independence.

We must now return to that main stream ourselves, taking up the story again in November 1827, shortly after the building of the *Experiment*, when Robert Stephenson returned from the Americas and gathered together the reins at Robert Stephenson & Co. With the *Experiment* his father had grasped the need to break away from the vertical cylinder convention, and the son took matters further. Writing in January 1828 to Michael Longridge, he said: 'I have been talking a great deal to my father about endeavouring to reduce the size and ugliness of our travelling engines, by applying the engine either on the side of the boiler or beneath it entirely, somewhat similarly to Gurney's steam coach.'

His first new design was demonstrated in the *Lancashire Witch*, an 0–4–0 built during 1828 for the Bolton & Leigh Railway, where he adopted the layout that Hackworth was to follow fourteen years later, with steeply inclined cylinders (approximately 40°) driving directly on to one pair of wheels, the others being coupled by rods; both axles were sprung with four independent plate springs. The boiler was unusual, representing an attempt to get better thermal efficiency than the large single flue offered without the considerable expense of installing a return flue, which was difficult to make and maintain; there were two separate single flues side by side, each containing its own fire, but leading into a common chimney. The *Lancashire Witch* gave satisfaction, and two more rather similar machines were built in 1828 and 1829, the *America*, to the order of the Delaware & Hudson Canal Company (who took delivery but never actually used the engine on a railway), and the Stockton & Darlington's no. 7 *Rocket*, which was an 0–6–0 with a return-flue boiler. Another two somewhat similar six-wheeled engines were also built in 1829 for tramroads in South Wales; and a final variant on the *Lancashire Witch* design was the *Twin Sisters*, built for the Liverpool & Manchester (who used it on construction work) in 1829. This carried the twin flue idea even further by having two entirely separate single-flue boilers side by side.

With these engines the Stephenson locomotive had reached a point of development where its layout was mechanically superior to its rivals, since the use of inclined cylinders allowed full springing without having to resort to expedients or to put up with excessive clearance volume. What the competition was in 1828 may be judged from looking briefly at two other designs built in that year. Firstly, two engines built by Robert Stephenson & Co to the designs of the French engineer Marc Seguin, for the Lyons and St Etienne Railway; these were four-wheelers with vertical cylinders placed between the wheels, and driving upwards on to a beam connected with the coupled driving wheels by a rod at each end (beam, connecting rods, and coupling rod thus formed a flexible parallelogram thrashing up and down, one on each side of the engine, which must have been fascinating to watch). Secondly, Foster & Rastrick of Stourbridge built two four-wheeled locomotives basically of *Puffing Billy* type and so still greatly influenced by stationary engine design. They had, however, the improvement of direct drive by connecting rods from the overhead beams to the wheels. One of these engines, the *Agenoria*, is now preserved in the York Railway Museum; the other, the *Stourbridge Lion*, was also delivered to the Delaware & Hudson and became the first locomotive to run on a public railway in the USA. Although Stephenson had come up with the best layout for the machinery, it was not yet seen to be decisively better. And Hackworth's boiler, though more expensive, was much better able to raise steam at the rate required for main line duty than the single flue type that everybody else was using.

It was at this point that the directors of the Liverpool & Manchester announced their proposal for a locomotive competition. The prize, and more particularly the chance of fame, glory, and future contracts, attracted a great deal of public attention and a large number of wouldbe entrants; as always, the number of these thinned away as the time shortened and in the event there were only three serious contestants. The conditions of the competition, however, were extremely onerous. The locomotive had to be fully sprung; it should not weigh more than six tons in working order, excluding tender, if carried on six wheels, or 4½ tons if on four wheels; steam pressure was not to exceed 50 lb per square inch, but the boiler was to be tested hydraulically to three times that amount; and the engine had to show itself capable of hauling, as a matter of regular practice, a load of three times its own weight at 10 mph. The further proviso, 'that the engine had to consume its own smoke', was put in deference to a recent Act of Parliament which had declared that future locomotives on public railways must do just that, in those words. This early (but by no means unprecedented) piece of smoke-abatement legislation had the effect of encouraging a change from the use of coal to the use of coke, which was more expensive but burnt cleanly.

Hackworth's entrant, the *Sans Pareil*, was a four-wheeled and smaller version of his *Royal George* design, with all wheels coupled, vertical cylinders at the leading end, and a small return-tube boiler. The use of springs thus involved a deterioration in cylinder performance which was made considerably worse during the trials by a crack in one cylinder casting which permitted live steam to blow through to exhaust. This, combined with a too-fierce blast and a troublesome leak in the boiler, caused the consumption of coke to become gigantic. The engine shared the basic weakness of its type, and although it had plenty of power and steamraising capacity it was mechanically unfitted for speeds as high as even 10 mph. To reduce weight while maintaining heating surface, each end of the flue was extended some 18 inches beyond the boiler in a tapered waterjacket. All the same, Hackworth had misjudged his weights and was several hundred pounds over the 4½-ton limit, so although he was permitted to compete he was technically ineligible for the prize.

Robert Stephenson's entrant, the famous *Rocket* (actually his second engine of that name, as we have seen), was a much better considered proposition altogether. It weighted only 4¼ tons, comfortably inside the limit, and it had two major advantages. Firstly there was its superior mechanical layout, which was that of the *Lancashire Witch*, inclined cylinders opposite the chimney, combined with the simplification brought about by the use of only one pair of driving wheels. Robert Stephenson had realized that although the conditions of the contest imposed a tight restriction on the locomotives' weight, they also restricted the loads they would be required

Figure 5 The *Rocket*, as entered for the Rainhill trials, with (left) a cross-section of the water-jacketed external firebox, and tubeplate

to pull, and so adhesion would not be a problem. The extra weight of a second pair of large wheels and connecting rods could therefore be saved, and in fact the *Rocket* was the first locomotive to be built with only a single pair of driving wheels. Even so, those wheels carried 2½ tons, which gave Hackworth's partisans ammunition later to point out that the *Sans Pareil*'s axleload was less than this.

The *Rocket*'s second major advantage lay in its boiler; the Stephensons now had acquired a commanding lead in this department of design as well. The shortcomings of earlier boilers were clear enough to anybody making an inspection of engines in constant service. Their capacity to supply steam was restricted, and as output rose the amount of draught required tore the fire and reduced efficiency. The return-flue type was somewhat better than the single-flue, but in both the wastage of heat was amply demonstrated by red-hot chimneys, quite apart from lumps of burning coal ejected at the chimney top. The problem was obviously how to extract more heat from the hot gases, and this could only be done by increasing the amount of heating surface, where heat could be transferred to the water in the boiler. The length of the boiler could not be much increased; therefore the amount of heating surface in the boiler's cross-section had to rise. The return flue and the twin flue experiment showed the way, and it was a simple geometrical fact that many small tubes offered a larger heating surface for the same gas area than one or two large ones. It seems to have been Henry Booth, the Treasurer of the L & M, who first pointed this out to Robert Stephenson, and certainly there was considerable correspondence between the two on the subject during the construction of the engine; but the mere thought of using multiple small tubes was no very startling discovery, and considerable problems had to be faced in execution. (At more or less the same time, as it happened, Marc Séguin in France had the same idea, and built a multitubular locomotive boiler somewhat on the lines of Hackworth's *Wilberforce* locomotives, though with the fire outside and underneath the boiler barrel, in a brick box which supported the boiler.) However, the fact remains that it was with the *Rocket* of 1829 that the modern locomotive boiler first took shape.

Not, however, its final shape by any means. The *Rocket*'s boiler barrel, like Séguin's, did not contain the fire. Twenty-five copper tubes ran through it from end to end. At the front, the bottom of the chimney was turned over and belled out to cover them; at the other end, they emerged adjacent to the external firebox. This took the shape of a copper waterjacket in the form of an inverted U, butting against the back of the boiler so that all the tubes emerged under the arch of the U, and the part of the arch below the boiler was filled up with firebrick. After 1831 a new firebox was fitted in which the waterjacket certainly extended around the other opening in the arch, with a hole let in for the firedoor, so that it then formed a figure like a cube with four surfaces; but possibly the original 1829 box had no rear waterjacket and filled in this space with firebrick also. Three external copper pipes, one to each side and one to the top, connected this waterjacket with the boiler in such a way that water heated by the fire syphoned back into the upper part of the boiler and was replaced with cooler water from below.

Although the details of its construction were therefore quite different, the *Rocket* had the essentials of the modern locomotive boiler; a firebox adequate for combustion and surrounded by water, combined with a battery of tubes which extracted as much heat as possible from the hot gases before they were exhausted up the chimney.

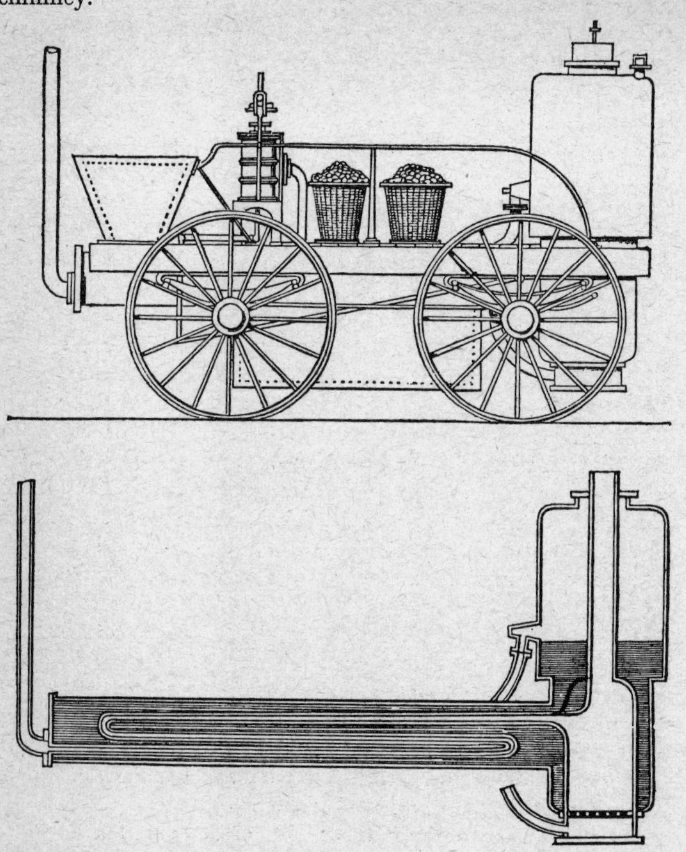

Figure 6 Braithwaite & Ericsson's *Novelty*, with a section of the boiler. The drawing shows neither the bellows for blowing the fire, nor the drive via bell cranks onto the wheels next to the boiler

The third important Rainhill contestant was Braithwaite and Ericsson's *Novelty*, very much the lightest entrant at under 3 tons. Its two designers both have a place in engineering history; John Braithwaite as the man who decided that railways in East Anglia should be of 5 ft gauge, and John Ericsson, a Swede, became better known for his marine work, including the first ironclad warship. Their *Novelty* was a very curious device indeed; mechanically it was fairly straightforward, consisting essentially of a four-wheeled platform with one axle driven by two vertical cylinders. No published drawing of the engine shows how these were arranged, but the notebook of J. U. Rastrick, one of the Rainhill judges, makes it clear that they drove downwards on to one arm of a bell-crank. The other arm of the crank then drove a nearly horizontal connecting rod which worked a crank axle; so the *Novelty* was not only fully sprung but was the first locomotive with a crank axle. Wood states that the second pair of wheels were coupled, 'when necessary', by a chain.

However, the real interest of the *Novelty* lay in its boiler, which was a complicated construction combining a vertical barrel with a horizontal one. The former contained a vertical firetube, whose diameter was reduced in the upper part, which led upwards to a door normally clamped shut and opened only to feed in coal. Air was blown in below the grate by means of a steam-powered bellows, not shown in the drawing, which blasted hot gases from the fire through the long S-shaped tube which coiled like an intestine through the horizontal boiler barrel and eventually out through a chimney more like an exhaust pipe. The object of the design, to extract as much heat as possible, was clearly the same as Robert Stephenson's, but the difference in execution is marked. The *Novelty*'s boiler must have been even more expensive to build than the *Rocket*'s, it added the complication of forced draught, and it suffered from the practical drawback that the blast had to be shut off before coke could be fed in (or else the fireman's eyebrows at the very least would be dramatically sacrificed). Cleaning the fire and the tube must also have presented problems.

The story of the Rainhill Trials, held in October 1829, has often been told. Suffice it to say that before a considerable crowd, who regarded the affair as a highly enjoyable sporting contest, the *Rocket* romped away with the prize, being the only engine to fulfil the terms of the competition. Hackworth under some difficulties put up a creditable performance in honour of the Shildon school of design, and the *Novelty*, though it had the sympathy of the crowd and managed to give the Stephensons one or two bad moments, had serious mechanical troubles and could not maintain its performance.

The company encouraged Braithwaite and Ericsson to persevere, and they built two more much larger engines on similar principles the following year, substituting an exhaust fan for the bellows blast; they cost vastly more than Stephenson's engines and proved failures, unable to maintain steam. All three of them were later purchased by St Helen's & Runcorn Gap Railway, which seems to have rebuilt them on more conventional lines: Rastrick's notebook shows a drawing of the *Novelty*'s boiler in 1833, with ordinary tubes and firebox, and apparently with blast instead of bellows.

So the main stream of locomotive evolution flowed through the *Rocket*, and during 1830 a number of basically similar locomotives were built. All except one were delivered to the Liverpool & Manchester Railway. One modification was made at once; in the *Meteor*, *Comet*, *Dart*, and *Arrow*, the cylinders were lowered to an almost horizontal position, while the *Phoenix* and *North Star* were provided with smokeboxes from the outset, the first time that this highly convenient aid to tube cleaning and general maintenance had been provided on any locomotives. Finally, with the *Northumbrian* and *Majestic*, the separate firebox was replaced by one contained in the rear section of the boiler barrel, completing the evolution of the conventional basic locomotive boiler. Each successive set of engines was also bigger, since experience rapidly showed that the *Rocket* itself was going to be too small for the regular traffic of the line. The *Rocket*'s cylinders, 8 in bore by 17 in stroke, gave way to 10 in by 16 in on the *Meteor* and 11 in by 16 in on the *Phoenix*, while the weight in working order by the time of the *Northumbrian* had just about doubled, to 8 tons. The earlier engines were altered as far as possible to bring them into line with the later ones, and the *Rocket* soon had her cylinders lowered to the near-horizontal position (where they remain on the original at South Kensington, but not on the various replicas that have been built from time to time, including one by Henry Ford), while all were soon given smokeboxes.

The odd man out among the *Rocket* class was the *Invicta*, built for the Canterbury & Whitstable Railway in May 1830. She had the same boiler and firebox arrangement, and the same steeply inclined cylinders, as the *Rocket*; but she was an 0–4–0 and the cylinders were placed at the opposite end, next to the chimney. This engine did not do a great deal of work, partly because the railway was steeply graded and mainly worked by fixed haulage, and about 1838 the external firebox was removed and replaced by a single fire flue, leading into a makeshift smokebox consisting of a drum with its flat surfaces horizontal. No doubt the reason for this was because the original firebox and tubes needed replacement. At any rate, shortly afterwards the *Invicta* was taken out of service, and ended up mounted on a pedestal in a public garden at Canterbury, where she still stands.

The L & M line was opened, in September 1830, with the fleet consisting entirely of all the *Rocket* type engines (except the *Majestic*) and these bore the responsibility of working the initial traffic. But Robert Stephenson was continuing to develop and improve his firm's designs; and as locomotives were fast becoming 'a regular article of commerce' several other builders, chiefly in Lancashire, began to produce them.

Stephenson's next move was the *Planet*, delivered to the L & M in October 1830. In power and size this was equal to the *Northumbrian*, and had a similar boiler; the distinguishing feature of the locomotive was that for the first time the cylinders were moved to their final place, more or less horizontal and in line with the driving wheels, below the chimney. With this alteration, the position of the driving wheels was correspondingly exchanged, and the *Planet* became a 2–2–0. The cylinders were placed between the wheels, achieving the neatness of arrangement akin to road steam coaches which Robert Stephenson had spoken of nearly three years earlier. The *Planet* design was readily adaptable to the 0–4–0 type, provided that the cylinders were set below the level of the front axle, inclined slightly upwards so as to be in line with the driving axle. The first two 0–4–0 *Planets* were the *Samson* and *Goliath*, weighing 10 tons in working order and built in 1831 for work on the Whiston and Sutton Inclines on the Liverpool and Manchester. From then till about 1835 many more of the class, both 2–2–0s and 0–4–0s, were built for various railways at home and abroad, including the *John Bull*, sent to America for the Mohawk & Hudson in 1831.

The other innovation of the *Planet* was that the locomotive was built on a separate frame. Previously, except on the *Novelty* and *Northumbrian* the boiler had always been used as the foundation of every engine, with wheels, cylinders, drawgear, and all other parts attached to it. Often enough there was some separate so-called frame provided of cast iron or wrought iron bar, to serve as a locating piece for the axle bearings, as on the *Rocket*, but this was structurally only incidental. The *Northumbrian* had a frame consisting of two iron plates standing on edge and set inside the wheels, but still little more than large locating pieces. With the *Planet* wheels, cylinders, and boiler were all attached to a strong frame, consisting of a wooden beam on each side of the engine, reinforced with iron plates inside and outside (and so called a 'sandwich' type frame). These beams lay outside the wheels. The cylinders' attachment to the frame was at first indirect, as they were bolted to the smokebox. The use of outside frames meant that the springs and bearings had, for the first time, to be placed outside the wheels; and the use of inside cylinders necessitated a crank axle for the driving wheels, which was a new development with a precedent only on the *Novelty*. Stephenson was always, with some reason, suspicious of crank axles; they were at that time difficult to make and liable to break. On the *Planet* and all subsequent engines he built until 1841 he provided separate sub-frames inside the wheels carrying additional bearings for the crank axle, so that in the event of fracture the wheels would still be firmly located and derailment would not follow; in most cases these inside bearings were unpsrung and carried no weight except in this emergency, though they did help to transmit horizontal forces between cylinders and axle.

Edward Bury, of Liverpool, built an 0–4–0 named *Liverpool* for the L & M during 1830 which established another school of locomotive design. Apart from having wheels of 6 ft diameter (much the largest yet used; Stephenson had not yet gone beyond 5 ft) this was similar in general layout to the *Planet* type, but with two main differences. Firstly, Bury used a boiler whose firebox was contained in a vertical barrel attached to the end of the main barrel. The top of this vertical barrel was closed by a dome: where it was joined on to the main barrel part of its circumference had to be cut away, so that for most of its height it was actually D-shaped. The firebox itself was therefore also D-shaped, and had a similar domed crown. This was a perfectly practical form of boiler, distinguished from Stephenson's by the fact that the latter's fireboxes (inner and outer) were flat-sided. However, it is sometimes difficult to distinguish the two varieties in pictures, especially as later on Stephenson (and other builders) carried the flat-sided outer firebox upwards into a flat-sided or Gothic dome, and this type of firebox, using a rectangular grate, should not be confused with Bury's, which had a D-shaped grate. It is unhelpful that many writers, including E. L. Ahrons, refer to Bury's as a 'haystack' firebox: haystacks can be either round or rectangular in plan.

The second trademark of Bury's design was his use of bar frames; he did not at first go so far as Stephenson in providing a frame capable of being regarded as a separate structure in itself, but he realized the desirability of relieving the boiler of mechanical stresses, and on the *Liverpool* the wheels were attached to a light frame built up from rectangular iron bars, two on each side. These were in turn bracketed to the boiler at smokebox and firebox. On later engines Bury carried one or more bars on each side to the front and rear, allowing cylinders and drawgear to be attached also. A number of Bury's locomotives were exported to America during the 1830s, and bar frames were adopted there as standard practice, spreading back across the Atlantic to Germany and Austria. However, in British practice frames built up from plates in the Stephenson tradition predominated and eventually practically monopolized domestic construction.

Bury's engine frames, and therefore bearings, were inside, so that there was not the protection against failure of the crank axle that the outside Stephenson frame gave. Other builders also provided variations on the *Planet* theme, often enough with an inside 'sandwich' frame extending the full length of the engine.

Although the layout of the *Planet* soon became the most popular, it did not entirely sweep the board. A number of builders experimented further with vertical cylinders, laid out in various ways. In most cases, in order to allow for springing, the cylinders drove one arm of a bell-crank, whose other arm was attached to a connecting rod as on the *Novelty*. Examples of these were the 0–4–0 *Caledonian* of 1832, built by Galloway for the L & M: Carmichael's 0–2–4 *Earl of Airlie*, built in 1833 for the Dundee & Newtyle (also the first British locomotive since Hedley's day to be fitted with a bogie); and some 2–2–0s built for the Dublin & Kingstown by Sharp, Roberts in 1834. The Stockton & Darlington obtained a vertical-cylinder 0–4–0 from R. and W. Hawthorn, named *Swift*, in 1836, whose cylinders drove directly downwards onto a dummy crankshaft set between the wheels, an arrangement doubtless intended to try and fit the machine for passenger service, for which Hackworth's lumbering 0–6–0s with overhanging vertical cylinders were unsuitable. Hackworth himself, on the other hand, built an 0–4–0 passenger engine, the *Globe*, in 1830, which had horizontal cylinders between the wheels, like the *Planet* type, but set beneath the footplate; this particular machine exploded in 1839 and was seen no more, but was the forerunner of a number of horizontal cylinder engines which Hackworth built for passenger work.

So far, in considering locomotive development, the account has been mainly confined to studying the general layout without consideration of much detail. With the appearance of the *Planet* type, some fixed principles began to emerge; and it is therefore a convenient moment to mention some of the individual parts, going back in time to see how their design had developed.

Starting with the cylinders, the first problem was how to provide guidance for the pistonrod; and in this matter there had been a curious regression from simplicity to complication. Trevithick in all his engines had a slidebar and crosshead arrangement; so did Murray, who followed him fairly closely, and so did George Stephenson at Killingworth, who copied Murray. Hedley, on the other hand, since he interposed a beam between cylinder and connecting rod, had a different arrangement. As built, his engines were fitted with strong posts at the chimney end, on which the two beams were pivoted; so the coupling between the other end of the beam and the pistonrod had to be made through a flexible knuckle joint, and the pistonrod had thus to be guided by a species of Watt Parallel Motion acting from a fixed point provided by two more rigid posts, one next to each cylinder. But the parallel motion swung from the end of a link attached to each beam, hung from the same pin as the connecting rod, a rather unsound arrangement. No doubt fairly quickly, these engines were rebuilt with slide bars supported by long diagonal stays, so that what had been the fixed end of each beam had to be supported by a rocking arm. This is so much simpler an arrangement that it is surprising that Hedley did not adopt it in the first place. It was used initially by the other builders of beam locomotives, Foster & Rastrick. Doubtless Hedley felt he should copy stationary engine practice. What is even more surprising is that when he came to build *Locomotion*, George Stephenson abandoned slidebars in favour of another variety of parallel motion, acting on a framework erected between the two cylinders; and the four similar locomotives he built for the S & D all had this complication. Hackworth's *Royal George* and *Victory* also used the parallel motion, in a slightly simpler arrangement. Robert Stephenson reverted to slidebars with the *Lancashire Witch*, and Hackworth with the *Sans Pareil*, whereafter the parallel motion was more or less banished from locomotive practice.

The development of valves and valvegear, up to the time of Nicholas Wood's experiments at Killingworth, has already been described. For some years practice remained on the same lines, with slip eccentrics driving slide valves with a moderate amount of lap but no provision for varying the point of cut-off, and therefore only allowing a limited amount of expansive working. On *Locomotion* only one eccentric was provided; it drove one valve directly, and the other through a separate valve rod leading from the eccentric at an angle of 90° from the first, with the motion transmitted to the valve by a bell crank. There was provision for moving each valve by hand to the correct position for starting by releasing a sprung catch, which would engage itself again as the engine drew away. The first attempt to allow for some control over the point of cut-off was made on the *Lancashire Witch* which was fitted with a rotating plug valve between the cylinders driven from one axle by means of a geared shaft passing through the boiler. This plug valve turned inside a sleeve which led to the ports of the cylinders and could be rotated through 90° in such a way that in one position it allowed a cutoff of something approaching 100 per cent, and in the other one of about 50 per cent. But this was a complicated arrangement which must have been difficult to keep steamtight, and although a simpler version using cams and mushroom valves instead of plug and sleeve was used on the Stockton & Darlington *Rocket*, with the Rainhill *Rocket* Robert Stephenson reverted to slide valves driven by two slip eccentrics, which arrangement was retained in the *Planet* type.

This, however simple to maintain, presented considerable problems to the driver. It was impossible to reverse the engine while in motion, which would have been a better method of stopping in an emergency than setting the primitive brakes on tender and train which were all that existed in the early 1830s; and it was a fairly formidable mathematical computation to consider in which position the valves should be placed in order to ensure the engine starting in the desired direction. Some men were better at it than others; we have a record from the early days of the Stockton & Darlington that the only driver able to reverse an engine in the dark was William Chicken. It was clearly highly desirable to do away with the slip eccentric for this reason, and provide some sort of arrangement whereby an engine could be reversed at any time by simply moving a single lever. It was not for some years that anybody came up with a method of doing this; before then, locomotives were normally fitted with two small handles attached to the boiler at the footplate and connected with the valve rods, allowing the position of the valves to be altered from the footplate. These handles were therefore in constant motion as the engine went along. In some cases the slip eccentrics were held in either the fore or aft position by lugs, and there was similar provision to allow these to be disengaged from the footplate so that the valves could be moved. These handles are usually shown clearly enough on drawings of early locomotives, but the details of operation are obscure.

The improvement introduced in the mid-1830s was the use of fixed eccentrics, combined with X- or Y-shaped 'Gabs' capable of being raised and lowered so as to engage with different pins. There were many variations on this gab gear. One used a single eccentric for each valve, driving a rod with a pin at the end, connected also with a rocking arm pivoted at the midpoint and another pin at the other end, which moved of course with opposite motion. At the end of the valve rod was an X-shaped gab capable of being moved from the footplate so as to engage with one pin or the other; since the opening at each mouth of the X was large enough to accommodate the whole throw of the eccentric from any position, one arm or other of the X would move the valve rod and the valve would be shifted automatically to its new position as the reversing lever was thrown over. In 1834 George Forrester of Liverpool came up with an improved version of the gear in which two eccentrics were used for each valve and the rocking arm dispensed with. The advantage of this was that the position of the valves in fore and back gear was not maintained at a separation of exactly 180° by the rocking arm, and it was therefore possible to set each eccentric so as to provide a certain amount of 'lead' in each direction. It was recognized as advantageous to admit steam to the cylinder slightly *before* the piston reached the end of its stroke, partly to cushion it and partly to ensure that the valve had time to open the inlet port widely before the power stroke began. But to do this it was necessary that the valve moved slightly more than 90° in advance of the piston, and therefore that the eccentric was set more (by the amount of lead) than 90° ahead of the crank. A slip eccentric or two separate eccentrics could be so set; a single fixed eccentric for each valve could not. However, even when the desirability of providing four eccentrics was recognized there was scope for considerable ingenuity in finding different methods of laying out the gabs and reversing gear. None allowed for variable expansive working, and fixed cut-off was still universal. For the further development of valve gear, see pp. 103–106.

Of boiler fittings, we have seen that the glass water gauge was due to Foster & Rastrick of 1829; this rapidly swept the board. Although very often two separate gauges were provided in case the glass of one burst, some builders still provided only a single gauge and two try-cocks to meet this emergency (indeed, this remained standard practice at Swindon until the end of the GWR). The water gauge was always provided with three cocks; two so that its connections to the boiler could be shut off, and a third leading to a blowdown pipe so that steam and water could be blown through every part of the gauge to ensure that the passages remained clear from dirt and scale, which could under certain circumstances give a dangerous false reading. Burst glasses have always been a chronic hazard, and it was many years before efficient protectors sheltered the crew from flying splinters, and longer still before the cocks leading to the boiler were customarily linked so that they could be shut off together by moving one convenient handle. It has fallen to the author only once as yet to have to cope with a burst glass on a gauge unprovided with this amenity; and struggling to shut off two small valves when one is blinded by a cab full of hissing high-pressure steam is an experience one may recommend to seekers after strange new thrills.

Pressure gauges were uncommon at first; the Rainhill conditions enjoined the fitting of a mercurial gauge, which was put onto the *Rocket* at least, alongside the chimney. Fifty pounds per square inch is equivalent to about nine feet of mercury, so that very much higher pressures could hardly have been accommodated inside the loading gauge. The alternative Bourdon pressure gauge, in which the indication is given by a dial across which a pointer is moved by the straightening out of a short length of coiled and sprung flattened brass tube as the pressure inside it increases, was invented by the Frenchman, the Comte de Pambour, and did not become common in Britain until the 1850s. Meanwhile, no means existed of telling what the pressure was, other than the behaviour of the locomotive, or the feel of the safety-valve springs.

Safety valves were of numerous types; that held down by an adjustable coiled spring was still popular, although the better practice was to make certain that the adjustments could not be carried out by the engineman, for painful and compelling reasons. Hackworth's lock-up valve, using plate springs held in a fixed frame, was also widely used. While on the subject of safety valves, one may remark that Pambour, who in 1832 conducted a series of scientific studies on the Liverpool & Manchester, calculated that not less than 25 per cent of the steam generated by the boilers of that railway's locomotives was blown to waste at the safety valves. It seems that the firmly held belief of the British main line steam locomotive fireman that he could not be said to be doing his job properly unless the safety valves were blowing away, and conversely that a plume of steam at the valves was necessary testimony to his competence and virility, has a long if dishonourable ancestry. The author prefers the economical French view that an open safety valve is a social solecism, like breaking wind, just as desirably brought under control without unreasonable delay.

Water was fed to the boiler by means of force pumps; generally there were two, one driven by each crosshead. A valve on the output pipe of the pumped water back to the tender if it was not required. Naturally, when the engine was not moving, water could not be supplied to the boiler, which might be awkward. On some early engines a hand pump was provided to use on these occasions, but as boilers grew larger and pressures rose manpower soon became useless for the task, and there was nothing for it but to make sure that an engine could always be run up and down over a few yards at least when necessary, or else to provide rollers to allow it to take gentle exercise without actually moving.

As a rule there were no ashpans, and the bottom of the grate was open, so that engines dropped live coals between the rails as they went along. It was customary to drop the fire at the end of a day's work by pulling up the firebars with a hooked rod and allowing grate, fire, and all to drop into a pit. It was not for many years that the fitting of ashpans became normal, and open-grate engines were still being built in the 1860s. At the other end of the gas path, fire-throwing at the chimney was a constant problem. The L & M commenced the task of developing an effective spark arrester in July 1830, and the search was still in progress at the end of the steam age.

After three years, the increasing size of the *Planet* type began to cause some difficulty. The L & M had been laid with wrought-iron rails weighing only 35 lb per yard, which were found to be sadly knocked about by four-wheeled engines weighing ten tons or so, more than half of which was on the driving axle, and the running of such engines was becoming rather unsteady. Furthermore, it was plain that larger and more powerful engines were still needed. So in October 1833 Robert Stephenson patented a new design, the first example of which, the *Patentee*, was delivered to the L & M shortly afterwards. It was a 2–2–2, whose features included a larger boiler with a longer firebox, and a steam brake, the first time this device had been used. Basically, it was an enlarged *Planet* type with an additional pair of wheels behind the firebox, intended to carry part of the load, improve riding by reducing the plunging of the rear end, and also to reduce the strain on the crank axle by allowing the driving wheels to be made flangeless. Possibly the *Patentee* was preceded by the rebuilding of two large *Planet*-type 0–4–0s of the Leicester & Swannington as 0–4–2s on similar lines; several *Patentees* were also built as 0–4–2s during 1833/4.

The increased size which the new layout permitted was soon demonstrated by another locomotive, the *Atlas*, delivered to the Leicester & Swannington in February 1834; this was an 0–6–0 weighing 17 tons in working order (without tender). With 4 ft 6 in wheels, 16 in by 20 in cylinders, and a grate area of 10 square feet, it was much the largest locomotive yet built, and of a size seldom equalled until the 1840s. Together with a smaller Patentee-type 0–6–0 built for the same company a few months earlier, it was in all essentials the prototype of the standard British inside-cylinder 0–6–0 goods engine, of which many thousands were built during the following 115 years. Considering the fact that the Rainhill trials had been held less than five years earlier, the giant strides which had been made in locomotive design in such a short period were truly amazing. Robert Stephenson & Co, in 1838 published detailed drawings of a 12-ton 2–2–2 *Patentee* with 5 ft driving wheels, 10 sq ft grate, and 12 in by 18 in cylinders, which they recommended for high-speed passenger work. Its cost at Newcastle was some £1,450 which compares well with the £400 or so asked for a Killingsworth-type locomotive seventeen years earlier.

A final development during 1833 was due to George Forrester, who built a number of 2–2–0s analagous to the *Planets* for the Dublin & Kingstown and other railways. He desired to make the machinery accessible, and therefore put the cylinders outside the wheels; and these were the first locomotives with horizontal outside cylinders conventionally placed (the *Rocket* type had had them below the firebox). Forrester's engines at this period were also interesting because, like the *Planets*, they had both inside and outside frames; however, the driving axles had bearings inside only, while the cylinders were attached *below* the outside frames. They suffered the same disadvantages as the inside-cylinder *Planets*, but their unsteadiness was even greater because of the placing of the cylinders further apart. By 1836, therefore, they had been rebuilt as six-wheelers, in which form they became the equivalent of an outside cylinder version of the *Patentee* type.

By 1834 new developments of design had proceeded about as far as possible, and it was necessary for locomotive engineers to turn their attention to questions of maintenance and construction. How to build these unprecedentedly large machines, how to keep them going, and how to improve their performances, had become pressing questions; and in any case there was something of a lull in the opening of new railways. The completion of the London & Birmingham and Grand Junction railways, the first long-distance main lines, was still several years ahead, but a rich prize awaited the builder whose engines were chosen for these lines, and this provided a further stimulus to consolidation and improvement. So with the exception of a few isolated experiments, no more changes in basic design took place until after 1840.

Like the engineers, the public also needed some time to adjust itself to this new phenomenon of railways, which had burst at last onto an astonished world. Henry Booth had something to say about this in his book on the Liverpool & Manchester published in 1830. On the final pages he wrote:

'Perhaps the most striking result produced by the completion of this railway is the sudden and marvellous change which has been effected in our ideas of time and space. Notions which we have received from our ancestors, and verified by our own experience, are overthrown in a day, and a new standard erected by which to form our ideas for the future. Speed, despatch, distance, are still relative terms, but their meaning has been totally changed: what was quick is now slow, what was distant is now near; and this change in our ideas will ultimately pervade society at large. Meanwhile, the genius of the age, like a mighty river of the New World, flows onward, full, rapid, and irresistible. The spirit of the times must needs manifest itself in the progress of events, and the movement is too impetuous to be stayed, even were it wise to attempt it. Like the Rocket of fire and smoke, or its prototype of war and desolation: though it be a futile attempt to oppose so mighty an impulse, it may not be unworthy of our ambition to guide its progress and direct its course.'

Prophetic words indeed.

CHAPTER FIVE

An Excursion into Manufacturing Technology

By the time the steam locomotive had become a commercial proposition, the Industrial Revolution had been in progress for a considerable time. Yet it was the stimulus provided by the spread of railways, causing an enormous increase in demand for iron products, with the need to develop methods of manufacture which could meet new demands of accuracy and strength, and the wealth generated by all these new activities, that decisively tipped the balance and turned Britain from an agricultural into an industrial nation; and it was because of Britain's leading position at the start of the world movement to industrialize that the country had the benefit of a century of unprecedented prosperity. The development of railway machinery, the progress of technical discovery, and the evolution in methods of manufacture, were to a large extent interdependent for fifty years from 1825, and it is useful to go back again in our chronological account in order to understand something of this.

Coal and iron were the two main sinews of railway development; the coal trade gave birth to the new means of transport by creating the need for it. But it was the iron trade that made it possible. Iron was far and away the most important metal to the railway engineers, and what they could do depended closely on what they could do with it.

Iron had been produced in small quantities for many centuries, by roasting or 'smelting' suitable ores in a charcoal furnace or 'bloomery'. Charcoal had to be used because it was almost pure carbon; any other fuel contained impurities, such as sulphur and phosphorus, which weakened the resulting iron. With natural draught and comparatively low temperatures, this process did not produce molten iron; instead, a spongy mass or 'bloom' of mixed iron and slag formed at the bottom of the furnace and could be drawn out in a lump. If this was hammered while still hot, the excess slag would be expelled and the relatively pure iron welded into a compact piece which could be further hammered, reheated as necessary, into the shape desired. This wrought iron was relatively soft; it could be hardened, and converted into a form of steel, by causing it to take up a certain quantity of carbon, either by longer and slower smelting of a few suitable ores, or by cementation, which produced a layer of steel on the surface of a piece of wrought iron left for a certain time in a slow charcoal fire. This steel could in turn be hardened and tempered by heating, quenching, reheating, and 'annealing' (slow cooling). It was an expensive process, but one well known to the Greeks and Romans, while the importance of being able to produce a sword that kept its edge and did not get bent or broken meant that iron metallurgy remained a living art even during the Dark Ages.

A suitable method for quantity production of iron was evolved in the blast furnace, which began to be used during the fifteenth century. By means of a forced draught from large bellows powered by a waterwheel, this accelerated smelting, and also made the process a continuous one, so that the furnace could be kept alight as long as it could be supplied with ore and charcoal, or, by 1800, generally ore and coke. Molten iron in amounts of hundredweights a day could be drawn off; the iron was run into branching channels formed in moulding sand in order to cool into ingots of suitable size, and observing the similarity between these channels and a sow suckling piglets, some artist with words named these crude ingots 'pig iron'. A blast furnace was large and expensive and needed to be worked by many men, and together with deep mining it therefore began the movement in which the increasing size of industrial units brought into being first the rich capitalist and later the joint-stock company. The legal and financial apparatus capable of administering the construction and operation of a railway thus existed from the eighteenth century, and especially after the further capital expenses following the introduction of suitable stationary steam engines.

In its molten state in the blast furnace, pig iron had taken up a great deal of carbon, and become brittle. There were some purposes for which it could be cast at once into its final shape, but the greatest demand was still for workable wrought iron. Another step was therefore needed to produce this, by decarbonizing it. At first this was done by the 'dry puddling' process, in which the iron was remelted in another furnace, away from contact with the fire, and an air blast passed round it to burn away the excess carbon. It also burned away a great deal of the iron. About two tons of pig were needed to produce one ton of wrought in this manner; furthermore, there was a limit to the size of an individual piece of wrought iron produced as it had to be manually handled in the puddling furnace, and not more than 40 or 50 pounds could be produced at one time. A greatly improved method of purifying the pig iron was invented by Joseph Hall about 1816 and became general practice during the early 1820s; in this 'wet puddling' process a quantity of iron oxide was added to the molten metal, removing the carbon and orher impurities by oxidation. Only 21 hundredweight of pig iron was then needed to produce a ton of wrought, and the size of the individual pieces could be increased to about 150 pounds if necessary. The price of the product naturally fell considerably, at the same time as steam railways began to spread.

Once a piece of wrought iron was removed from the puddling furnace it had to be hammered to a usable shape and quality. Hand hammers were soon outclassed, being able to deal with quantities of only a few pounds at a time. Helve-hammers, lifted by water power and falling by gravity, came next, and hammers driven by steam engines followed. During the 1790s John Wilkinson of Shropshire had a hammer driven by a Watt engine with a head weighing 7½ hundredweight, falling through a height of 2 ft 3 in; it was lifted by a cam, fell by gravity, and was capable of some thirty strokes a minute, so it was an apparatus of fairly considerable power. But by the 1820s there were hammers in use weighing 6 tons. James Nasmyth invented the steam hammer, powered directly by steam working on a piston connected to the hammerhead, in 1839, and soon developed it so that it was not only lifted but driven downwards by steam; hence its power could be infinitely graduated, from an impact too feeble to crush an eggshell to a blow of many tons.

The purpose of this hammering was twofold. As it emerged from the puddling furnace, wrought iron still contained a lot of slag, which had to be hammered out. But, just as important, wrought iron is unusual in that its structure is extremely fibrous, like a piece of wood; and working the metal, by hammering or rolling while hot has the effect up to a point of improving its strength and quality by arranging these fibres in parallel. For certain purposes, for example coupling and connecting rods, the iron could be hammered or forged into its final shape; but for most purposes it needed finally to be rolled. Initially hammered into a roughly oblong bloom, it would then be squeezed (while still hot) between power-driven rollers into a shape roughly 1 in by 6 in by anything up to 15 ft long. This 'puddled bar' was the raw material from which wrought iron in any of the thousand and one shapes required by the market could be produced, by reheating and rerolling between appropriately shaped rollers.

Fortunately wrought iron has another property, that it can be readily hammer-welded at a reasonable temperature; consequently it was possible to produce rolled sections larger than the puddled bar. Sheets or plates of wrought iron were made by piling lengths of puddled bar on top of each other, heating the piles, and then rolling them down to the required thickness. By arranging the bars in the piles so that alternate layers were at right-angles the plate could be given a cross-ply grain structure, with considerable increase in strength. Although wrought iron in fairly small cross-sections could be produced readily, and rails (either of parallel or, using eccentric rollers, fish-belly section) of about 35 lb per yard could be rolled in lengths of 15 to 18 feet during the 1820s, it can readily be imagined that the production of plate was a more formidable proposition. The size of the plate was determined by the size of the rolling mill and the difficulty of assembling a pile of puddled bars to be heated and rolled, and it was a matter of some complication to consider how to increase it. The largest plate capable of being produced by the Bedlington ironworks, which supplied Robert Stephenson & Co., in 1831, was only about 3 feet by 4 feet by $\frac{3}{8}$ in, and twenty-two were needed to form a *Planet* boiler. By the 1850s very much larger plates were being produced, but in the early days this was a serious limitation.

One interesting wrought iron product was tyres for wheels, which were first used apparently by Hackworth in the late 1820s. The earliest tyres, applied to locomotive wheels, were plain hoops shrunk onto a cast iron wheel and flange; but soon George Stephenson's associate, the ironmaster William Losh, produced a wrought iron tyre with flange. In each case the tyre was made up by a length of rolled iron of appropriate section bent round and welded; naturally the weld was a source of weakness. However, a means of producing weldless tyres was invented by F. Bramah in 1844. A long strip of wrought iron was bent and coiled in a tight spiral in such a way that the thickness of the tyre was the width of the strip; it was then finished in a true circle by special rollers.

Steel was not much used at first in railway engineering; the major exception was for springs. It was made in a crucible by Huntsman's process, which involved melting down steeled wrought iron in the classical way by prolonged heating with charcoal. The slag was thus driven off and a homogeneous metal resulted, but its quality was rather uncertain and it was still very expensive.

Cast iron was capable of improvement by various processes which reduced its brittleness by removing much of the carbon contained in the metal; one, due to Réaumur in 1722, involved heating the castings bodily for several days in contact with powdered iron ore. Another process was developed in America in 1826. Both are still in use, together with others invented subsequently. By such treatments it was possible to make castings of iron which, though not with the same tensile strength as wrought iron, were as strong in compression and adequate when used in the thick sections common with castings for such functions as cylinders, valve chambers and steam chests, frame stretcher blocks and even axleboxes. The high-duty castings which are nowadays used for such demanding tasks as petrol engine crankshafts are made by processes of recent invention which give a cast iron of strength approaching that of steel; during the nineteenth century, however, 'malleable' iron castings were regarded with some reserve, and not used where considerable or repeated stresses were met with. In any case they were rather expensive, and could not be made very large. The choice between malleable cast iron and wrought iron or other metals usually depended, other things being equal, on the shape of the article required and the feasibility of building it up from wrought iron sections.

Two other metals of importance to early railwaymen were copper and brass, both of which had been familiar to metalworkers for thousands of years. Copper was produced by smelting, like iron; however, the metal was much softer and more ductile than iron, and although its characteristics also varied according to the proportion of other constituents in the metal, it did not exhibit anything like the same divergence in behaviour in its cast or wrought forms. Copper plate was produced by rolling castings of any suitable size, and used mainly for fireboxes or to form tubes and pipes. Copper does have the undesirable characteristic, unlike wrought iron, that its brittleness increases markedly as it is worked, but its ductility can be restored by heating the final shape and then annealing it.

Brass is an alloy of copper and zinc, or rather a series of alloys differing in strength and hardness according to the proportions of the two metals. In mid-nineteenth-century practice tin was used to the exclusion of most of the zinc, and it might be more accurate to speak of bronze, though this was not done. Like copper, brass is considerably more expensive than iron, and has better resistance to corrosion. It is very readily worked, and with a fairly low melting point it is easy to cast into fairly complicate shapes. Hence it was, and still is, much used for small details such as taps, plugs, and fittings. It also has a low coefficient of friction on iron and good resistance to wear, and so by the time steam locomotion began to spread brass was almost universally used in all kinds of bearings, in contact with steel or wrought iron pins or journals, superseding plain cast iron. By mid-century it had been superseded, for axle bearings, by white metal, an alloy of lead, tin, and antimony, very weak mechanically and with a low melting point, but with even lower friction and better resistance to wear. A thin pad of white metal was therefore let into the brass casting which formed the body of the bearing. Nowadays this bearing is set in a cast iron axlebox; nineteenth-century practice was for the axlebox to be brass also. To this day all three metals are still used in different sorts of plain bearings, cast iron for cases where cheapness is all and little is required in the way of performance, brass for connecting rod little ends and wagon bearings, and generally white metal for connecting rod big ends, coupling rods, and locomotive and carriage axles.

Three methods existed for joining different pieces of iron: riveting, bolting, and welding. Welding by the heat of a gas flame or electric arc, which raises the local temperature of the metal above melting point, did not exist until much later: the first primitive electric welding, using a carbon arc, was demonstrated in 1885, and oxyacetylene methods were experimented with around the turn of the century. But neither system was much used until the 1920s. In the 1820s welding meant pressing two pieces of wrought iron together while they were at welding heat, white-hot and beginning to sparkle. The pressure could be from hammerblows or a steady squeeze (as in a rolling mill producing plate). Clearly welding of this kind was not the reasonably convenient affair capable of being carried out by portable equipment that it is today. Small things could be welded together by a blacksmith, provided that they could be brought to the right heat on his fire and carried to the anvil while still hot. Any other kind of welding was a factory job, where special large heating furnaces and lifting equipment could be provided. It was customary in the 1830 for Sharp, Roberts & Co. and certain other builders to weld axle guard plates to locomotive frames, and frames themselves at least in the region of cylinders and driving wheels were often welded up out of the small plates available. It was not, according to E. L. Ahrons, until 1868 that plates large enough to form one-piece frames began to be delivered from the rolling mills. Only wrought iron could be pressure-welded in this way; the method did not work with cast iron or steel, because it depended on the fibrous nature of the metal.

Riveting was the most common method of fastening two pieces of metal together. It had the advantage that it was not necessary to heat the pieces to be joined, which might therefore be as large and awkward as necessary, provided only that they could be held together correctly and in firm contact while the riveting was going on. In its original shape, a rivet is a length of rod which has had one end forged into a mushroom-shaped head, rather like a bolt without a thread; it is brought to red heat, driven through a hole passing through the two pieces of metal joined, and another mushroom head formed on the protruding plain end either by hammering or by a hydraulic press. During this time it is essential that the rivet be held firmly in place, otherwise it will be loosened; it is also essential that the two pieces of metal are forced together, otherwise the rivet will swell out between and separate them. A rivet can never be a tight fit in a hole, because it has to be driven through while hot and is bound to shrink on cooling; its strength depends on the way it clasps the two plates together along its length, and constant racking strains will tend to loosen it. Once loosened, it will fail progressively. Many rivets are therefore needed to form a strong joint. Even so, if joints in a main locomotive frame between cylinders and driving wheels were riveted, the rivets would soon tend to work loose because of the considerable and rapidly alternating racking strains at every stroke of the piston. Boiler plates had to be riveted together because of the difficulty of pressure-welding them; fortunately, although these joints have to resist considerable forces, they are not racking forces, being generally constant and not alternating, although as we have seen it was a recognition of the undesirability of imposing additional stress on these joints that led Robert Stephenson to provide a separate integral frame in the *Planets* and subsequently. A riveted boiler joint also needed to be caulked with some suitable material such as oakum to prevent leakage, though before long accuracy of fitting was improved so that the caulking material could be mainly provided from the boiler plate itself, hammered *in situ* while cold.

Riveted joints did have the advantage over welded joints in one way, since they could be visually inspected from time to time for integrity, while a welded joint might not show any visible defect before failure, which was clearly undesirable in boilers. It was not until the 1940s that the welding of steel boiler and firebox plates began to be practised to any extent on British railways, and riveting remained the standard method right up till the end of steam construction.

There remained the third method, the common or garden nut and bolt, which of course has a very important part to play in engineering. It is akin to riveting in that the fastening passes through a hole, but it has two considerable advantages. One is that the pieces can as readily be parted again, for maintenance or any other reason. The other is that this temporary method of fixture can be made very much stronger than riveting: if the main length of the bolt is threadless, and turned very accurately to an exact diameter corresponding with the diameter of accurately bored holes, so that the bolt then becomes a 'driving fit' in the hole, it will have a very good resistance to racking strains. Fitted bolts of this kind have therefore always been the standard method of attaching such parts as cylinders and slidebar and motion brackets to locomotive frames. It is of course essential to make sure that the nut does not slacken off; in the early days locknuts were sometimes used, but these do not work well and the standard method of fixing the nut on large bolts has always been to pass a tapered cotter pin through both nut and bolt, the cotter itself being secured either by a split pin or a combination of a drawnut on a threaded extension of the cotter and a split pin.

Brass and copper could be joined by riveting or by bolting, but not by welding. (Copper welding is possible, but needs great quantities of heat and very careful treatment during and after the process, and is again a quite recent development.) On the other hand, both metals can be joined by another method, brazing, which by means of a conveniently manageable application of local and not very intense heat to the joint, with a suitable flux and a brazing metal with a low melting point, gives a joint composed of the brazing metal which adheres to the parent metal by forming an alloy with it at the surface. It is a process akin to soldering, but giving a stronger join which can stand greater heating.

The manufacture of tubes, at the time Robert Stephenson first employed them on the *Rocket* in 1829, was dependent on brazing or welding. The tube was formed from a suitably sized length of strip metal, iron, brass, or copper, bent to shape round a forming bar and with the seam joined by welding or brazing. The earliest boiler tubes were of copper, but these were found to wear very quickly from the action of hard fragments of coke drawn through them by the blast. In 1833 tubes made from hard brass began to be used instead, with much better results. Iron tubes also began to be used in the 1830s, but brass remained the commoner material right through the nineteenth century, even though iron slowly gained ground. Seamless tubes were unknown until 1838, when Charles Green patented a process for their manufacture in brass and copper. The method was rather like that used to make lettered rock: a suitably proportioned casting was made with a hole in the middle but very much greater in cross-section, and drawn down to the size of the finished tube by a process of stretching. Iron was too strong to be dealt with then in this way, and seamless wrought iron tubes never existed. The first seamless steel tube was made by the Mannesmann process, patented in 1885; a very ingenious method which involves hot steel rod being passed between rollers whose axes are inclined to each other in such a way that the rod while still between them is forced forwards onto a piercing-bar, and then expanded to the desired size. Tubes cannot be made in any length by this process, naturally, since there is a limit imposed by the length of the piercing-bar; but the length of a locomotive boiler is within the capabilities of the system. It was the ease of manufacture and cheapness of steel tubes made by this method which caused them to be adopted in preference to brass tubes by main line railways during the twentieth century, although brass tubes could still occasionally be found on locomotives on industrial and minor lines even during the 1950s, and some brass-tubed engines are probably still steaming. Brass resists corrosion better than steel; but this is not much of an advantage in practice, since it was the custom on principal railways to extract the tubes every five years or so to allow the boiler to be internally examined, and steel tubes will generally last this period. Once extracted, the ends of the tube are damaged and it cannot well be reused even if otherwise sound, although some railways made a practice of cropping off the damaged parts and then placing the tube onto a Procrustean machine which would stretch it to the original length. Another advantage of steel tubes is that the corrosion from which they suffer mainly takes the form of deep electrolytic pitting here and there on the water side; hence, when one pit has eaten right through the metal, the tube gives warning of impending failure by starting a slow leak. A brass tube, on the other hand, lasts a long time but when it does go goes with a bang.

Fastening the tubes to smokebox and firebox tubeplates caused some problems at first, but three methods were used from the earliest days. The tube could be riveted in position, with a protruding length hammered down over the surrounding metal; this method is generally called 'beading', and Robert Stephenson in giving an account of building the boiler of the *Rocket* called it 'clinking'. Alternatively, a tapered steel ferrule could be driven into one end of the tube, with the effect of expanding it and holding it firmly in place. A third method was introduced by Dr Church, an amateur engineer in Birmingham, who in 1833 invented an expanding mandrel by which the end of a tube could be expanded manually *in situ* in the tubeplate. (Some years later the good doctor was killed by the explosion of a four-wheeled 0–2–2 tank engine with 6 ft 2 in driving wheels that he had built himself, which is a cautionary story perhaps, but his expanding mandrel is evidence of a degree of engineering skill that deserved a better fate.) All three methods of fixing tubes are still in use today, sometimes in combination. A fourth and recent method is to weld the tubes in, generally only at the firebox end; this certainly prevents leakage but makes it somewhat more difficult to take them out again.

The very earliest fireboxes were of copper, as we have seen. However, iron was the traditional material for the large fire flues in earlier boilers, and copper was then as now an expensive metal, so it is not surprising that during 1830 a determined attempt was made to use iron plates for firebox construction. But it was not a success. As already explained, wrought iron is fibrous in structure, and between the threads of iron are threads of slag; furthermore, there is no very rigid consistency in the quality of the metal from plate to plate or even from part to another of the same plate; while the slag inclusions which help to explain its good resistance to corrosion have the effect of making wrought iron a relatively poor conductor of heat. Hence there was great trouble with blistering and cracking, and although a few wrought iron fireboxes lasted well there was absolutely no way of knowing why, and how to make others like them. The early L & M records show that many fireboxes lasted only 5000 to 8000 miles before having to be scrapped and renewed, while some were still in good order after 20,000. So in May 1832 Robert Stephenson & Co. gave up the attempt, and standardized on copper for fireboxes, and other manufacturers followed suit. Copper remained the normal material from then until the end of steam in Britain, although latterly this was increasingly due to conservatism; steel eventually made a perfectly satisfactory material and became standard in American and German practice after the 1920s.

The production of cylinders had been one of the worst difficulties faced by the pioneers of stationary steam engines. Even in Watt's time, there were at first no means of boring out the cylinder casting to a truly cylindrical shape, and one cylinder made for him in Glasgow by the best workmen available varied in diameter by $\frac{3}{8}$ of an inch at different points. This kind of accuracy was good enough for cannon, the only things for which large holes had previously been needed in big castings, but rather unsatisfactory for a steam engine. The best an engineer could do was therefore to provide a piston which left as few gaps as possible, and plug those with hempen rope, felt, or oiled rags. With atmospheric engines the cylinder was usually pretty full of water anyway, and as the stroke was vertical the piston itself lay level and the water lying about helped to provide the seal by keeping the packing damp and swollen. With Watt's separate condenser the cylinder became dry and so the old methods would not do at all; still less would they have done as steam pressures and therefore cylinder temperatures started to rise with Trevithick. Smeaton, who was himself responsible for an improved pattern of atmospheric engine, assured Watt that neither the tools nor the men existed who could make a cylinder accurate enough for Watt's engine. However, John Wilkinson in 1775 developed a boring-mill capable of meeting Watt's demands, in which the cutting tool was held on a rigid extensible arm while the cylinder casting was revolved round it, again held very accurately. Watt's partner Matthew Boulton was delighted, and wrote: 'Wilkinson hath bored us several cylinders almost without error: one of 50 inch diameter doth not err the thickness of an old shilling in no part.' By the time of the locomotive, the technology thus existed for sufficient accuracy in the cylinders themselves; the difficulty was more in the foundry, since from the time of Matthew Murray and the slide valve the cylinder and valve chest were cast in one piece, and relatively complicated and unmachineable passages for steam had to be provided in the casting itself. This led to dangers like those which befell the *Sans Pareil* at Rainhill, where due to the displacement of a core in the mould, what appeared superficially to be a sound casting was only card thin in one part, leading to a burst and leakage of steam.

Hemp piston packing continued to serve, with increasing difficulty, until the development of the metallic piston ring. This was a most important innovation, which originated on railways and has since been adopted on every kind of piston engine. John Ramsbottom introduced piston rings of rolled brass at Crewe in 1853/4 and announced the success of his experiments to the Institution of Mechanical Engineers in a paper read on 3 May 1854. In this he claimed a saving in weight of the ringed piston over its hemp-packed equivalent of no less than 31 pounds. David Joy, the following year, came up with a cast iron double-coil piston ring, turned from a cast iron cylinder, which wore much better than the brass ring. In both types, two or three rings lay in slots cut round the edge of the piston, and were held against the cylinder wall by their own elasticity. Hemp packing continued a while longer in piston and valve rod glands, until displaced by asbestos packings from 1879 onwards. These enabled glands to withstand the higher pressures used in steel boilers.

One-piece cast iron wheels had, as we have seen, superseded

wooden wheels on railway wagons during the third quarter of the eighteenth century. They had a good run of fifty years and more, but were outclassed by the needs of the steam railway. They had been considerably improved, especially by a process of chilled casting; this involved the use of a mould part of which, forming the tyre and flange of the wheel, consisted of a cast iron ring set in the moulding sand. The molten iron in contact with this was cooled rapidly, and this chilling caused local hardening just where it was needed; it also helped to drive a nail into the coffin of the tramplate because hardened wheels used on plateways cut grooves into them. But the stresses set up in the casting tended to weaken it, and made more certain the development of built-up wheels. In locomotive practice, as we have seen, Hackworth developed a wheel composed of cast iron segments with a wrought iron tyre band, but this was not followed by others, who after 1828 changed to other types of built-up wheel. At first the spokes and usually the nave and rim were wooden, with a wrought iron tyre forced on; in most cases the spoke to which the crankpin was attached was reinforced by a circular strap attached to all the other spokes. These part-wooden wheels needed to be strongly made, and were, so the Liverpool & Manchester found, very expensive. After 1832 they were abandoned.

The all-metal built-up spoked wheel took a very large number of forms; textbooks like Wood's *Practical Treatise* (1838 edition) and Brees's *Railway Practice* (1847) devote entire folding plates to show their variety. Locomotive and carriage and wagon practice were on similar lines, though naturally the former needed greater strength. One early patent was due to William Losh in 1830. Most designs had in common the use of cast iron naves and wrought iron spokes; the rim might be cast or wrought, and the tyre was always wrought. One of the odder designs was Dierck's patent wheel, which was cast iron throughout, except for the tyre, which was of wood! The segments were bolted to the rim, and the specification called for African hardwood, understandably.

The greatest variety of design was in the spokes, which might be lengths of tube or solid rod cast into the nave, or built up out of interlocking patterns of bar in various sections, formed into wedge-shaped figures. The methods of fixing varied; best of all was that the solid spokes be cast into the nave, and the tyre shrunk onto the rim. The latter was usually bolted in some way onto bar spokes, and cast onto tube or rod spokes. The practice of attaching the tyre to the rim not by shrinking it on, but by means of bolts passing through the tyre and so weakening it, sounds pernicious but was in fact widely adopted. It had fallen into some disfavour by the middle of the century following a series of breakages, but as late as 1874 some elderly passenger coaches were still running round on wheels of this kind. On Christmas Eve of that year one of them, through the breakage of a tyre, caused the appalling accident at Shipton on Cherwell, on the GWR near Oxford; following this, which killed thirty-four and was the worst accident that had till then happened on a British railway, such wheels were purged as far as passenger vehicles were concerned, though even now one may sometimes see a privately owned freight wagon with them mouldering in a siding. On the other hand, some tyres even on locomotives were secured by a stud passing through the rim and into (but not through) the tyre; this less objectionable type of wheel was made into the 1920s and was in use into the 1950s on, for example, the leading bogies of certain LMS *Patriot* 4–6–0s, nominally rebuilds of older engines.

After the mid-1840s there was something of a reaction away from the built-up wheel, especially in locomotive practice, and a reversion to solid centres. Some were made in malleable cast iron; others were made of solid wrought iron according to a method patented by John Day in 1835 but not widely used until the patent expired some ten years later, when the use of the steam hammer greatly aided manufacture. These one-piece wrought iron wheels were forged in a die with a shaped hammer; they were excellent and strong, but exceedingly expensive, and could not be made large enough for locomotive driving wheels. Built-up wheels also continued in use, particularly on rolling stock, and it was not until the twentieth century that there came to be any real standardization of methods of making wheels. The most popular carriage wheel during the nineteenth century, valued because of its quiet running and still occasionally to be found on preserved stock, was Mansell's, patented in 1848; its centre was solid and built up of tapered wooden blocks, retained by iron rings to which they were bolted, and compressed tightly by the tyre. Nowadays all wheel centres are steel castings, which began to be used for the purpose in the 1880s. Separate tyres are still normal, but one-piece cast steel wheels with tyre included also began to be made in the 1880s and are very common, being standard for freight vehicles in America (complete with chilled hardening of the tyre area). A case of the wheel turning full circle.

Axles were a difficult problem at the start of the railway age, and their breakage was all too frequent. They were invariably of wrought iron, but a number of basic mistakes were made. As late as 1835, Dempsey in *The Practical Railway Engineer* made clear that it was only beginning to be appreciated that fractures often started from cracks at a change of section, and till then it was quite common for wheels to be set on a small part of the axle of larger diameter than the rest, and for the journal to be turned down to a smaller diameter, so that several changes of section were introduced, and right at the most critical place, the nave of the wheel. The wheel itself was forced onto the axle, and secured from rotating on it, by a tight-fitting key in a slot cut into both wheel and axle.

Locomotive crank axles were a special and even more difficult problem, though builders often preferred to face the additional risks of fracture than adopt outside cylinders; it was a matter of judgment, but the main argument in favour of inside cylinders was that they gave smoother riding, because the leverage causing the engine to 'nose' was nearer the centreline and therefore less powerful. Crank axles during the early nineteenth century were invariably forged out of solid wrought iron, often reinforced with hoops round the web of the crank or bolts through the pin. Built-up crank axles, assembled from separate parts fitted and keyed together, appear to have originated, in Britain, at Crewe under Webb in the 1880s. There is a report from America dated 1850 that the Baltimore & Susquehanna Railroad used crank axles of solid cast iron to their entire satisfaction, never having had a breakage. Warren, in his centenary history of the firm of Robert Stephenson & Co., treats this as a Yankee tall story, which it may have been; but it is by no means impossible. British locomotive engineers criticized Americans at this time for using cast iron too much: but it was good stuff, probably better than British, due to the advances in cast iron metallurgy that have already been mentioned. The Norris engines on the Birmingham & Gloucester had cast iron slidebars, for example; the scoffers pointed in scorn, but we have no accounts of any breaking.

To complete an account of early nineteenth-century railway manufacture one must give some idea beyond a description of the materials available and how they affected design practice, and have a look at the tools that were available to do the work and the premises in which the work was done. On the second point, Warren quotes Sir George Bruce, speaking as President of the Institution of Civil Engineers in 1887, who had entered the service of Robert Stephenson & Co. in 1837 as an apprentice. At that time the company's works at Forth Street, Newcastle, employed 400 men and in that year built twenty-nine locomotives, which sold at an average price of some £1300.

> In 1837 there were no small planing or shaping machines: there was only one slotting machine, the use of which was very restricted. Wheels were driven onto their axles by sledge hammers, wielded by strong arms alone. Steam hammers were of course unknown, and only hand labour was available for the ordinary work of the smith's shop and boiler yard, with the exception of the punching and shearing machinery. Riveting by machinery was unknown. It is scarcely credible, but it is a fact, that there was not a single crane in Robert Stephenson's shop in 1837. There were sheer-legs in the yard, by which a boiler could be lifted onto a truck, and there were portable sheer-legs in the shop, by the skilful manipulation of which, at no little risk of life and limb, wonders were done in the way of transmitting heavy loads from one part of the shop to another.

Another brief quotation—Sir Joseph Whitworth (1803–87), the maker of machine tools, speaking of the time at the start of his career when such terms were normal usage: 'What exact notion can a man have of such a size as a "bare sixteenth" or a "full thirty-second"?'

These two short items, like a pair of snapshots, give us an instructive insight into workshop practice in the early railway age, though Whitworth's complaint might have been made much more recently. The effect of railway development in bringing about improved standards of accuracy in manufacture was less direct than its effect in bringing about improvement in materials, since railway machinery tends to be less demanding in the former respect; but even if the development of machine tools moved in parallel and not in series it is worth a brief account here.

We have mentioned Watt's difficulty in getting his cylinders accurately bored. The production of accurate flat, or even convex, metal surfaces was little easier, and much was owed to Henry Maudslay (1771–1831), a pupil of the lockmaker Joseph Bramah. In 1794 Maudslay first applied a slide rest to a lathe; a simple step, but one which by enabling a man to rest and hold firm and steady a cutting tool began to turn the lathe into a precision instrument instead of a method of free self-expression like the potter's wheel. He went on to produce the planing machine, of which Joseph Whitworth said in 1856, 'Thirty years ago the cost of labour for facing [i.e. producing an accurate flat surface on] a surface of cast iron, by hand, was 12/- per square foot. The same work is now done by the planing machine at a cost for labour of less than a penny a square foot.' Another thing that seems basic to us now was the introduction of the first standard specification for screw threads, by Whitworth in 1841; before that nuts and bolts were made for each other individually, and there was no guarantee that they would be interchangeable even when the same size.

Apart from hand tools, the only machines available to work in railway workshops in the 1830s and 40s were thus the lathe (which produced accurate round surfaces, even complicated ones, including male screw threads), the planing machine (which produced accurate flat surfaces), the boring machine (which can be regarded as a specialized form of lathe producing a concave curved surface, and which was soon modified so that it was the cutting tool which moved, and not the workpiece), small drilling machines, and the slotting machine. Let James Nasmyth of the steam hammer, who invented the latter, describe its function.

> One of the most tedious and costly processes in the execution of the detail parts of machinery is the cutting of cotter slots in piston rods, connecting rods, and of key recesses in shafts and axles. This operation used to be performed by drilling a row of holes through the solid body of the object, and then chipping away the intermediate metal between the holes, and then filing the rude slot so produced into its final form. The whole operation, as thus conducted, was one of the most tedious and irksome jobs that an engineer could be set to, and could only be performed by those possessed of the highest skill. What with broken chisels and files, and the tedious nature of the work, it was a most severe task to the very best men, not to speak of the heavy cost in wages. In

order to obviate all these disadvantages, I contrived an arrangement of a drilling machine, with a specially formed drill, which at once reduces the process to one of the easiest.

Naturally the variety of machines at the engineer's command was improved and widened considerably. One of the most important advances, the development between the forties and sixties of machine tools capable of being adapted to mass production, like the first turret and automatic lathes, was due to the needs of gunmakers such as Colt in the United States and the Royal Ordnance Factory at Enfield, and passed the railways by. But the basic heavy equipment improved steadily throughout the wrought iron age. It is perhaps worth noting that grinding (except for sharpening tools) was much less important then; the only available grinding materials, such as emery or sandstone, were irregular and inconsistent and tended to embed themselves in the metal, leading to wear and tear in service. More accurate results could be obtained by the use of, for example, the planing machine. It was not until the development of better abrasives, including synthetic silicon carbide, in the 1890s that grinding became precise enough to be widely useful.

The replacement of wrought iron by mild steel, which was a gradual process lasting from the early 1860s to 1900 or so, together with the associated improvements in machine tools and the development of high-speed cutting tools in special alloy steels, revolutionized railway engineering (as it did heavy engineering in general). Mild steel was a completely new material, at first produced in the Bessemer Converter, in which the carbon and slag was burnt out of pig iron by a blast of air passing through the molten metal. Bessemer first announced his process in 1856, but it was some ten years before it became reliable; some ten years later it was supplemented by an alternative, Siemens's open-hearth process. Both produced a similar product, whose nature could readily be modified by adding appropriate substances to the relatively pure and unadulterated molten steel which emerged. Mild steel was homogenous and consistent, unlike wrought iron; it could be cast or rolled into bars, rails, plates, and any other section with equal satisfaction; it was tougher, harder, and much more resistant to wear than wrought iron. Finally, because of its ease of manufacture and the fact that it could be produced in increasingly large unitary amounts while the capacity of the rolling mills had expanded correspondingly, there were no longer any significant technical reasons why plates could not be made as large as needed, at any rate in railway practice. The extent of the mild steel revolution must therefore be borne in mind when comparing design and practice before it and after.

For a short account of iron and steel manufacture in general, the reader is referred to W. K. V. Gale's book on the subject in this series.

CHAPTER SIX

Locomotive Development, 1835-1860

When we left the account of the development of the locomotive at the end of 1834, the most important recent move had been the introduction of the *Patentee* type by Robert Stephenson & Co. In those days the law was somewhat kinder to the inventor (or the company wishing to steal a march on its rivals) than it is now, when it would not be possible to patent anything so intangible as the positioning of another pair of wheels behind the firebox; but so it was then, and other builders wishing to take up the idea had to pay royalties. The virtues of the layout were such that they were more or less forced to do so. By 1840 there were some 630 locomotives at work in Britain, over 420 of which were six-wheelers, and the vast majority of these were *Patentees*. The principal exceptions were the few 0–6–0s by Hackworth and others. *Patentees* had also been exported, to France, Russia, Belgium, and Germany (where they included the famous *Der Adler*).

The various builders nevertheless brought in some modifications to the design. One change was a gradual lengthening of the distance between the centre and rear axles, in the interests of better weight distribution; for the rear wheels of the original engines of the type had been very lightly loaded, having been provided mainly to relieve the strain on the crank axle. This change also enabled a larger firebox to be conveniently provided, since it sat in the gap between these two axles. But as boilers grew in size so the weight on the front pair of wheels, which were set well back and behind the cylinders and smokebox, increased. We have seen that the original 2–2–2 *Patentee* layout was very soon added to by an 0–4–2 version; the first 2–4–0 example of the type appeared in 1837, with some engines built by Robert Stephenson & Co. for the Paris & Versailles railway. It was not until 1839 that any of this particular variant were used in Britain.

So far all inside cylinder locomotives with front coupled wheels, whether they were 0–4–0 *Planets* or 0–4–2 or 0–6–0 *Patentees* suffered one considerable inconvenience. In order for the connecting rods to clear the front axle, the cylinders were set below it. This meant that whenever attention to the front axleboxes was needed, the whole of the motion had to be taken down before the locomotive could be lifted off its front wheels. This drawback could be avoided by using outside cylinders; and another reason to use them was provided by the continuing suspicion of crank axles. The first locomotives to be built as conventional outside cylinder six-wheelers thus appeared in the late 1830s, commencing with two 0–4–2s by G. and J. Rennie for the London & Croydon railway in 1838, where they were used as banking engines on the New Cross incline. In 1839 Stirling of Dundee built a number of outside cylinder 2–2–2s for Scottish lines.

The users of outside cylinders remained in a small minority, however. The arguments against them centred on the greater difficulty of keeping the cylinders hot and preventing condensation due to their exposed position, and the unsteady running which it seemed that they caused. The most important variety of outside cylinder engine in the early 1840s was the 'Crewe type' 2–2–2, due to Alexander Allan of the Grand Junction railway. The original inside cylinder 2–2–2s of this line suffered a large number of broken axles while rounding the sharp curves of the triangular junction with the Liverpool & Manchester at Newton-le-Willows, and Allan determined to try and cure the difficulty by rebuilding some of them with outside cylinders and plain axles. The result was entirely successful, and a considerable number of similar engines were built at Crewe from 1843, when the locomotive works there were opened. Joseph Locke took them with him to France, where he was building the Paris to Le Havre line, and they proved very popular there also, where they were known as *Buddicoms.* A 2–4–0 variety for freight traffic was built at Crewe from 1844.

The principal resistance to the advance of the six-wheeled locomotive came from Edward Bury, who apart from building engines for several other quite important lines had the contract to provide motive power for the London & Birmingham Railway. By 1841 the L & B had eighty-eight Bury locomotives, fifty-eight 2–2–0s and thirty 0–4–0s, all of his characteristic inside bar-framed design with D-shaped fireboxes. Bury's defence of his ideas was impassioned.

He said that four-wheeled engines were cheaper (which was true), and also that they were less liable to derail and break down, while being lighter they need not be so powerful. They certainly were not so powerful; two or three were commonly needed for each passenger train, and four for freight; on one windy day it is recorded that seven had to be used to get a 45-wagon goods train along. One trouble was the restriction on heating surface imposed by the use of the D grate. In order to prove his case regarding safety, Bury carried out a rather hair-raising demonstration in May 1842 with 2–2–0 no. 18, cutting through the front axle on a lathe with a ⅜ inch wide cut so that only an inch of metal was left. He then stormed off down the line from Wolverton, and naturally enough the axle broke; but he continued nevertheless to Roade (7¼ miles), reversed through the crossovers, and came back again. Part of the secret was a very tight and rigid coupling between engine and tender. The fact remained that there were several nasty accidents following axle breakages on Bury's engines, and in any case however strongly built they were too small for the traffic. In 1845 the London & Birmingham changed its locomotive policy, and Bury commenced to build six-wheelers like everybody else. A place remained for the 0–4–0 tender engine of Bury's design for some time to come—the Furness Railway had some built as late as 1861—but not on main line work.

Although their line died out, the Bury family of locomotives were not without relatives during the 1840s, and perhaps the most interesting of these were the American 4–2–0s of the Birmingham & Gloucester. American practice at this time was still much influenced by British, and particularly by the *Planets*, though it was beginning to draw away and follow its own line of development, to cope with local conditions which included rough tracks and steep gradients. The Birmingham & Gloucester included the well-known Lickey incline, 2½ miles of 1 in 37, which was reasonably steep even by American standards; and doubtless influenced by the confidence with which American builders said their engines could cope, the company ordered fourteen from Norris of Philadelphia, delivered in 1840–41 (another nine were later built in Britain). They can be regarded as greatly enlarged outside cylinder *Planets*, with a bogie instead of a fixed front axle, and they resembled Bury's engines in having bar frames and the characteristic boiler with D grate. They were still quite small, weighing only some 13 tons, but gave good service (alongside more conventional machines) in both general mixed traffic and Lickey banking service before finally being converted into saddle tanks.

The next important new type of locomotive was the subject of another Stephenson patent; the 'long-boiler' engine of 1841. It had been observed that, as they grew larger, the *Patentee* type engines tended to be front-heavy, while when they worked hard a great deal of heat was wasted by passing through the boiler. Smokebox temperatures of 600°F were quite common: more than hot enough to melt lead. Stephenson therefore resolved that it was necessary to lengthen the boiler, so that this heat might be more effectively used in the tubes; and in order to get a better weight distribution and avoid lengthening the wheelbase, it would be necessary to place all three axles in front of the firebox. At the same time, having been impressed by the steadiness and reliability of Bury's engines (within their limits), Stephenson gave up the outside frames with additional inside members and bearings for the crank axle that he had introduced with the *Planets*, and adopted a single inside plate frame. It was beginning to be realized that the double framing and multiplicity of bearings, intended to guard against the consequences of axle breakage, was actually rather a menace, since the frames inevitably flexing in service the bearings would get out of line and place extra strain on the axle. The first locomotives of 'long boiler' type were a series of 2–2–2s of 1841, but the following year a 2–4–0 version appeared, and in 1843 an 0–6–0, and all were built in some number. With the 0–6–0 the cylinders were for the first time placed above the level of the front axle, obviating at last an ancient inconvenience. Outside cylinders were also applied to the design, with a 2–2–2 in 1844 and a 2–4–0 in 1845; a few rather odd outside cylinder long boiler 0–6–0s were built for the Stockton & Darlington in 1847, but although this pattern became the standard and highly successful European goods engine and could still be found running in France and Spain after 1945, it was never much liked in Britain.

Indeed, the long boiler engine did not really do very well at home, and after a few years' popularity was obsolescent by 1847. It had its drawbacks. The most serious of these was its unsteadiness. There was a considerable overhang at each end, which meant that it tended to nose from side to side, and rather badly at more than 45 mph. Another was that the firebox could not be made large enough for more than modest sustained power outputs, otherwise the rear overhang would have become too great. With the 0–6–0s, working in slow freight service, neither of these factors mattered very much, and its greater economy and better mechanical layout explain why the six-coupled long-boiler engine so greatly outlasted the other varieties. But in endeavouring to cure the defects of the type as they appeared during the early 1840s, some useful advances were made.

First of all, one tenet that locomotive designers had clung to zealously from the very earliest days had been the importance of a low centre of gravity. It was felt that engines with a high centre of gravity were bound to be unsteady; this did not have to be proved, it stood to reason. They would surely roll and buck, and display a desire to lie on their sides when going round curves. Only John Gray of the Hull and Selby Railway disbelieved this, and no other engineer followed him. People looked askance at such of his machines as his 5 ft 6 in 0–6–0s with boiler centres as much as 6 ft above the rails, and passed by on the inside of the bend (if the engine was moving) or the outside (if it was standing still). Other designers went to considerable trouble to keep their boiler centres as low as possible, not more than about 5 ft 6 in and sometimes less than 5 ft above the rail; they would build oval boilers, or provide recesses in the boiler shell to accommodate the tops of the wheels, and even sometimes, as on the famous *Cornwall* of the L & NWR in 1847, have the boiler below the axle entirely, with a recess in the steam space to accommodate it. Yet there was a puzzle. The express long-boiler engines, with a commendably low centre of gravity, were still unsteady at speed. Why?

Faced with this conundrum, engineers began to realize that part of the reason for unsteadiness had to lie elsewhere, and to accept that there was a need which they had hitherto disregarded to balance the reciprocating weights of pistons, crossheads and connecting rods, and (where they existed) the rotating weights of coupling rods. At speed, the disturbing effect of these unbalanced movements was considerable and quite sufficient to explain the oscillation observed with the long-boiler engines. It was a matter of rather more difficulty to decide quite how the balancing should be done, as the mathematics involved were somewhat complicated and the whole theory of dynamic balancing by no means understood. However, some success was achieved by various rule-of-thumb methods during the 1840s, and after the Frenchman le Chatelier had published his theory of balancing in 1849 the results could be predicted with some confidence.

In an effort to improve matters, the cylinders of the express long-boiler locomotives were moved rearwards, first in some outside cylinder 4–2–0s for the Great North of England in 1845, and later in some outside cylinder 2–4–0s for the York, Newcastle & Berwick in 1848. But the improvement obtained in this way was not great, and a further cloud fell on the type after a long-boiler 2–2–2 engaged in a demonstration before the Gauge Commissioners in 1846 left the road and turned over.

Balancing, in fact, was improved too late to save the main-line long-boiler design, although some success was achieved with two interesting 4–2–0s built for the London & Birmingham in 1846. These had three cylinders. Both outside cylinders drove cranks set on the same quarter, so there was no tendency for the engine to 'nose'. The middle cylinder, twice the size of the others, drove on a crank set at 90° to them; thus although the balancing was not perfect, it cancelled out all but straight fore-and-aft forces. It was, of course, well appreciated that perfect balance of reciprocating weights could only be achieved by equal and opposite movement of other reciprocating weights, and some attempts were made to do this with levers and even with opposed pistons (i.e. two pistons moving in opposite directions in the same cylinder—Bodmer, 1845). The first man to build a four-cylinder locomotive with both cranks on the same side set at 180°, so that the pistons on each side balanced each other, was the Englishman John Haswell of the Austrian State Railways, in 1861. This became the standard four-cylinder layout thereafter.

Another type of engine, nearly contemporary with the long-boiler design, was Crampton's. Patented in 1842, this set about improving the express locomotive in a different way. Greater boiler power and efficiency, a lower centre of gravity, and larger driving wheels, were desired; retaining a short wheelbase was considered unimportant. Crampton's answer was to place the driving wheels behind the boiler, so that the wheels could be as large as necessary without causing any great rise in the centre of gravity; indeed, the boiler could be lowered compared with other engines. With outside cylinders set well back, normally two carrying wheels, and a long wheelbase, Crampton engines rode very well, especially as Crampton was one of the first to appreciate the need for proper balancing. With their large driving wheels—generally seven or eight feet in diameter, at a time when ordinary locomotives had wheels of between five and six feet—they were also fast, and the layout allowed room for a big enough firebox and long enough boiler to give adequate power and efficiency. The weakness of the design was limited adhesion weight, since it was not easy to load the driving wheels very heavily; their long wheelbase also made them slightly suspect from the point of view of the civil engineer, although the only Crampton which was positively convicted of causing damage to the track was the very large 6–2–0 *Liverpool*, built for the London & North Western in 1848. Cramptons did very well on the continent, and ran for many years in France and Germany (the SNCF still has one as a workable relic); their reception in Britain was however rather mixed, although some ran into the 1870s on the South Eastern Railway. Probably the basic reason for this was no more than the often repeated British dislike of the unconventional in locomotives.

With the long-boiler type falling from favour for passenger work, the need remained for engines of greater power for main-line duty, and during the late 1840s and 1850s the standard express locomotive was a 2–2–2 developed out of the *Patentee* design, with one axle behind the firebox, but generally larger and better proportioned. Double frames were commonest, though there were many builders who used inside plate frames; inside cylinders were normal, though outside cylinders were not infrequent. The problem of overloading the front axle (which was set behind the cylinders) remained a difficult one, but as boilers and particularly fireboxes grew larger the centre of gravity of the engine tended to move rearwards and improve weight distribution over the three axles automatically. Even so, the first four-axle locomotives began to appear in the late 1840s, all express 4–2–2s of unusual power. Most important were Daniel Gooch's *Iron Duke* class of 1847 on the GWR broad gauge, whose prototype, a 2–2–2 built the year before, had broken its front axle due to overloading. But there were others, including one for the L & NW by Stephenson in 1848, though this was really a long-boiler 4–2–0 with an additional pair of wheels behind the firebox.

Some noteworthy mainstream designs of the period certainly include these of Archibald Sturrock, the first locomotive engineer of

the newly-built Great Northern Railway, whose raison d'etre was to provide a better route from London to the north-east. Sturrock began the policy of having larger and more powerful engines than the competition, which remained an East Coast tradition right down to the end of steam. He started with basics, remarking that 'the power of an engine is measured by its capacity to boil water', and went in for large boilers and fireboxes, more or less doubling grate area, and high pressures. He was the first to use steam at 150 lb per square inch. Yet, apart from one bogie 4–2–2 he built in 1853, he did not find it necessary to go beyond six-wheeled express locomotives. McConnell of the L & NWR, with his *Bloomers* of 1851, also produced an unusually powerful 2–2–2, and with less regard for the low-centre-of-gravity shibboleth.

The 2–4–0 locomotives, both inside and outside cylinder, also grew in size, and began to be used for express as well as goods and semi-fast work. But the engine with coupled wheels suffered from a disadvantage; with relatively soft and inconsistent wrought-iron tyres, the wheels soon wore to unequal diameters. Imperfect balancing made matters worse, and it was not uncommon for coupled engines running fast to bend their rods and come to a sudden grinding halt. With the availability of steel for tyres at the end of the 1850s, matters changed somewhat, since tyre wear could be greatly reduced; the first successful four-coupled express engines were Beattie's 2–4–0s of 1859 on the London & South Western. But steel cut both ways, since it allowed axleloadings and thus adhesion to be greatly increased, and this helped the single-wheel engine to survive well into the twentieth century. It did have the advantage that no power was required to keep the coupling rods spinning.

Daniel Gooch and others had experimented with wrought iron tyres with steeled faces in the 1840s; these were made by incorporating a steel bar in the pile from which the tyre was rolled. But they were not very successful; they were brittle, and the faces so hard they could not be turned on a lathe. According to Ahrons, the first all-steel tyres, by Krupp of Essen in 1851, were made from castings of crucible steel, heated and rolled. Various modifications of this method were most widely used at first; later, castings were replaced by forgings. But the British steel industry lagged badly in producing steel tyres; as late as 1930, for instance, the firm of Kerr, Stuart found it necessary to go to Belgium for reliable cast-steel tyres.

During the 1850s the 0–6–0 type improved its position as the standard goods engine. The long-boiler design lasted longest in this version, as we have seen. The first 0–6–0s with inside cylinders and rear axle behind the firebox, combined with an inside plate frame, which were even more truly the prototypes for a century of British goods engines, appeared on the Leeds & Thirsk line in 1848. All that really happened afterwards was that the machine got bigger (within limits).

Tank locomotives, carrying coal and water supplies on the same frame as the boiler, remained unimportant before 1860, although with the increasing number of short branch lines after the 1840s a need was felt for small, light, and economical motive power to work them and carry their often disappointingly thin traffic as cheaply as possible. Light inside or outside cylinder 2–2–2Ts were commonly built for this purpose; often some superannuated main line engine was rebuilt as a tanker (as happened to the Birmingham & Gloucester's Norris 4–2–0s). For heavier duty, shunting or freight traffic on short industrial lines, somewhat larger engines were built. A species of long-boiler 0–6–0T was popular for a long time, and in fact well outlasted the tender variety; the National Coal Board still had a few as late as 1950. The Bristol & Exeter had some unique broad gauge 4–2–4Ts with 9-foot driving wheels, built for express trains in 1853. Tank engine water supplies were at first carried in well tanks beneath the footplate, or in saddle tanks slung across the top of the boiler; the first side-tank engines were some 4–2–2Ts for the Waterford & Kilkenny in 1846.

One interesting byway was explored by a few who built light rail motors, though these remained rare. The two best-known examples were both by W. B. Adams: the *Fairfield*, a six-wheeled broad-gauge car for the Tiverton branch of the Bristol & Exeter, with a vertical boiler and single driving wheels at one end, capable of carrying fifty-eight passengers and hauling two light trailers, and the *Enfield*, for the Eastern Counties' Angel Road to Enfield branch in 1849, a four-wheeler which was smaller (only containing thirty-four seats) but more powerful, capable of hauling two four-wheeled coaches.

One of the most helpful steps towards increasing power and efficiency during the 1840s was the invention, at last, of a satisfactory valve gear which not only enabled easy reversing and reasonably good valve events at a fixed cut-off, like the various forms of four-eccentric gab gear already described, but also enabled the cut-off to be varied while running and thus at last to extract more energy from a given quantity of steam. Like many great discoveries, the Stephenson valve gear was more or less accidental. It originated with William Williams, a 'gentleman apprentice' draughtsman in Robert Stephenson & Co.'s works, during 1841. He was experimenting on paper to try and find an arrangement more mechanically sound than the X-shaped gab engaging with two pins alternately, working as already described (p. 70). This layout had the disadvantage that unless the reversing lever was firmly home, the drive of the valve was disengaged and damage could easily result; while reversing was sometimes hard work, if the valve needed to be moved a great distance during the relatively small final travel of the reversing lever. Besides which, the thing was altogether inelegant. Purely as a mechanical simplification, Williams came up with the idea of a slotted link, along which one end of the valve rod could slide. One end of the link took its motion from the fore and the other from the back eccentric; by raising or lowering the link, the valve would be moved steadily to its new position. William Howe, a patternmaker at the works, assisted with the working out of the design, and suddenly at some stage somebody realized that if the position of the reversing lever was moved slightly while the engine was running, the effect would be, by shortening the stroke of the valve, to reduce the proportion of the stroke of the piston during which live steam was admitted to the cylinder. The long-desired object of a mechanically sound variable cut-off, which had eluded Nicholas Wood at Killingworth, Robert Stephenson with the *Lancashire Witch*, and the many other designers who had sought it, had suddenly been attained. Well might Robert Stephenson, when the matter was reported to him, reply 'if it answers, it will be worth a Jew's eye and the contriver of it should be rewarded'. The first locomotive fitted with the Stephenson Link valvegear was a 2–4–0 turned out in 1842, and the effectiveness of the arrangement was at once evident.

It was, of course, patented; and in order to get round the patent various subterfuges were, of course, adopted. Daniel Gooch, on the GWR, evaded royalties by one simple change in the layout which he adopted in 1843. In the Stephenson arrangement, the valve rod was fixed, and the reversing lever raised and lowered the eccentric rods and the link: in the Gooch gear the link hung from a fixed bearing and the reversing lever raised and lowered the valve rod. The letter of the law was thereby satisfied, and technically Stephenson's patent was not infringed. Alexander Allan, at Crewe, devised an arrangement by which the reversing lever raised the valve rod at the same time as it lowered the eccentric rods and link, and this had the same desired legal effect. Since with Allan's gear the link was straight, while with Gooch and Stephenson it had to be curved to the radius of the rod or rods moved by the reversing lever, his arrangement is sometimes known as the Allan 'straight-link' motion. Of the three types, the Stephenson gear was perhaps the best and became almost universal in Britain and America for the second half of the nineteenth century; it is still by no means rare. Gooch's layout was at a mechanical disadvantage, since the angularity given to the valve rod caused backlash and increased wear and tear in the link, and in Britain it was more or less confined to broad-gauge engines. Allan's was mechanically sound, more compact and easier to manufacture than any, though rather more complicated than Stephenson's; it was fairly widely used, and even now one occasionally comes across it. It had one minor advantage, in that with Stephenson gear the weight of the link unless counterbalanced tends to draw the reversing lever forward, but Allan gear is already balanced and the driver's job is thus physically easier.

Numerous other types of valve gear were experimented with; but the only other wholly satisfactory design, which vastly predominated all over the world in twentieth-century practice, was almost a contemporary of Stephenson's in its original form, having been invented by the Belgian Eugene Walschaerts in 1844. Except for one engine, it was unknown in Britain until 1890. It has two major differences from the Stephenson gear; it uses only one eccentric (or return crank) and the reverse motion of the link is obtained by allowing it to rock on bearings at its midpoint; while a fixed and unvarying amount of lead in either direction is obtained by taking part of the motion of the valve from the crosshead, by means of a combination lever. This compares with the performance of the Stephenson gear, in which as the cut-off is reduced, the amount of lead increases; and unless certain modifications are made, by the time cut-off is 25 per cent or less lead is excessive and steam enters in front of the piston too long before it ends its stroke. Cut-offs of this order were not however practical with engines working on saturated steam, and this helps to explain the changeover to Walschaerts with superheating after 1910.

Among other changes in detailed design from 1835 to 1860, one of the most visible was in boiler cladding. Until about 1838, boiler barrels were generally lagged with stained and varnished wooden battens, bound with iron or brass bands (thus causing some to believe that engines at this period had wooden boilers), while the outer fireboxes were usually left uncovered. This caused wastage of heat, and so from 1839 it became customary to clad the firebox also; at first only the rather easier flat sides but later throughout. The wood was generally highly polished, and to protect this finish from heat a layer of felt was next laid beneath the wood. However, rain got in between the battens and rotted this. From 1847, therefore, builders began to cover wood and felt with sheet iron, which has remained in use ever since; although in subsequent practice the wood lagging beneath was replaced by a magnesia plaster, or ultimately by tailored asbestos or fibreglass mattresses wired into place.

Both sorts of 'haystack' firebox, Bury's round or D-shaped and the square-grate 'Gothic' pattern, disappeared from new construction about 1848. Bury's design suffered from the limitation of grate area due to the waste of space outside the round part of the grate; both were more expensive to construct than the round-topped outer firebox, which became universal thereafter until the end of the century, and remained popular beyond that time. The inner fireboxes, except for Bury's, never originally had round or domed roofs, but flat tops or 'crowns' which were reinforced by girders in the waterspace the same length as the firebox itself. With the increase in size of boilers during the 1840s these girders developed into bridge-like supports carried between both sides of the outer firebox, their ends resting on brackets, supporting the crown by staybolts several inches long which allowed water to circulate between crown and girder. Like the stays between the sides of inner and outer fireboxes, these were screwed through the plates and then generally riveted over as well, then as now; though occasionally nuts were used instead of riveting and nuts were always used to secure the crown stays to the roof girders. Grates were generally level; the first locomotive with a sloping grate, intended to allow a driving axle to be placed more readily beneath it, was a 2–4–0 for the South Eastern in 1856.

One oddity of boiler design was that until 1839 it did not seem to occur to anybody that boilers expanded when hot; they were always securely fastened to the frames at each end, and engines must therefore have arched their backs slightly whenever they raised steam. In that year Isaac Dodds, of the Sheffield & Rotherham railway, introduced the arrangement universal ever since, of fastening the boiler securely only at the smokebox end (where in any case it had to be attached to cylinders and steampipes), and allowing it to slide in a bracket mounting at the firebox end (where this movement was easy to allow for).

Boiler pressures had reached a norm of 70 psi by 1841. The pioneers of higher pressures were John Gray (of the high centre of gravity) on the Hull & Selby, who was using 100 psi in the early 1840s, and Sturrock of the Great Northern, who used 150 psi in 1850. General practice lagged some 30 psi behind these pioneers. Increased pressures depended in any case on variable-expansion valve gear; there was not much point in putting them up while engines still had to work at long fixed cut-offs.

During the 1850s a determined effort was at last made to break away from the use of coke as a fuel, and adopt coal, which was very much cheaper. The difficulty was the statute enjoining that engines should 'consume their own smoke'. It was well appreciated that, in order to burn without smoke, coal needed a freer supply of air than coke, above as well as below the grate, with a larger space for flames to circulate; and that the normal small box which did quite nicely for coke was quite unsuited for coal. Some hair-raising methods for increasing the amount of air circulating above the fire were tried out, including one by Samuel Hall in 1841 which involved passing a number of boiler tubes right through the smokebox and into bell-mouthed airscoops at the front of the engine. Rushing along through the (sometimes freezing) breezes, cold air would pour through the boiler, cooling it nicely, and so to the firebox. From time to time no doubt an anxious fitter would try to staunch the leaks caused by differential expansion of the tubes. Other systems involved baffle plates in the firebox; Beattie on the L & SWR had two fireboxes, coal smoke from one passing through a coke fire in the other. McConnel on the L & NWR in 1852 appreciated the importance of a big firebox, but final success in burning coal sufficiently smokelessly was achieved on the Midland railway by a series of experiments between 1856 and 1860. These produced the solution still used today, with a brick arch across the front portion of the fire to deflect flames through a longer path before they reached the tubes, combined as a rule with a deflector plate above the firedoor to project additional air on to the surface of the fire, and sufficient firebox volume. Once the thing had been done, everybody followed suit and coke burning soon ceased. Only the Great Western, burning South Wales coal, had a somewhat different practice; this fuel is much nearer to pure carbon than any other British coal, and hence behaved more like coke. The GWR adopted the brick arch, but needed less air through the firedoor, and found it could get sufficient power out of smaller fireboxes than other railways.

The action of the exhaust steam in the smokebox, and the reason why it induced a draught, was not well understood at this time; indeed, locomotive men were slow to learn from scientists, and it was only towards the end of the steam age that draughting really began to receive proper scientific attention. It sufficed for the practical man that the blast worked, never mind why. One popular belief was that it was because each puff of exhaust acted like a gaseous piston, pumping flue gases up the chimney between each beat. For this reason a number of builders, including particularly Messrs Beyer, Peacock, used a form of chimney tapering inwards towards the top, theorizing that as the steam condensed so it would occupy a smaller volume. For the same reason, the blast pipe was usually placed high up, practically at the base of the chimney. The rival school, who believed that flue gases were drawn away by some form of friction with the exhaust, were eventually proved more nearly right. But the whole matter was dealt with on a rule-of-thumb basis, and new locomotives were experimented with individually until the size and position of blastpipe that gave satisfactory steaming was hit upon. In service, from that day to this, further surreptitious modifications were made from time to time by engine crews, who knew well that the steaming of a difficult engine could always be improved by putting in a 'jimmy' to reduce the area of the blastpipe nozzle, and so sharpen the blast at the expense of increasing back pressure in the cylinders, and sending up the coal bill.

The earliest *Patentees*, or some of them, had had steam brakes working on the wheels of the locomotive, but these were not continued. General practice, with tender engines, was to have no brakes at all on the locomotive and to depend on the handbrake fitted to the tender. The reason for this was mainly a desire to avoid the strain on the crank axle imposed by the grip of brakeshoes on the wheel. Sometimes the driven wheels of coupled locomotives were braked, which met the point about the crank axle but then imposed a strain on the coupling rods, which were also looked at with some anxiety; while braking the carrying wheels was seldom resorted to. Indeed, in the case of tank engines, particularly those with single driving wheels, quite often the engine had no brake at all, and reliance was placed on the guard's handbrake and a code of whistle signals. In an emergency, the driver could always throw the engine into reverse, which was a spendid gesture of romantic desperation but had little effect in stopping a train moving at any speed. The importance of having satisfactory and powerful brakes was forcefully driven home from time to time; but not until the 1850s did it become at all common for locomotives to have brakes on their own wheels, either hand-operated or steam-powered. Daniel Gooch tried to solve the problem in his broad-gauge GWR 4–4–0 saddle tanks of 1849 by fitting sledge brakes, bearing directly down on the rails between the coupled wheels; these were effective enough as brakes, but exhibited a dangerous tendency if they were applied too hard to lift the engine off the rails. Occasionally sledge brakes were used on coaching stock (D. K. Clark's *Railway Machinery* of 1855 shows a van so fitted). No means existed during this period for the driver to apply any brakes on the train; this was the responsibility of guards and brakesmen.

Little has been said about locomotives built for Brunel's seven-foot gauge, mainly because they formed a group which died out completely with the abolition of the broad gauge in 1892 and had in any case become moribund long before. No important new broad-gauge design appeared after the 1850s, and right up to the end the principal expresses were worked by 4–2–2s which were direct descendants of Gooch's *Iron Dukes* of 1847. No real advantage was ever taken of the engineering possibilities of the broad gauge; what eventually killed it, and its fate was clear enough once the Gauge Commission had reported to Parliament in favour of standardization on the 4 ft 8½ in gauge in 1846, was the commercial drawback caused by the break of gauge. Before 1846 there was certainly some highly original thinking on the subject of broad gauge locomotive design;

unfortunately most of it, largely Brunel's, was entirely unsound and right from the start the best broad gauge locomotives were those which adopted standard gauge design principles, at first on a bigger and better scale.

Right at the end of the period, locomotives intended for service on gauges of less than four feet or so began to appear. (Steam power had long been used on railways of a gauge slightly less than 4 ft 8½ in, including the Middleton line.) It is sometimes put about that the very first locomotives to work on the narrow gauge (in its modern sense, meaning about three feet or less) were the Festiniog Railway's England 0–4–0s of 1863, but this is by no means so. Zerah Colburn, in his *Locomotive Engineering* of 1864, lists several previous examples in industrial service. There were several 8-ton 0–4–0s working on a 2 ft 6 in gauge line at Willenhall Furnaces which was 1½ miles long and had a grade of 1 in 30; Isaac Boulton had a mile-long 2 ft gauge line near Wigan, with a 1 in 50 grade and a tunnel 6 ft 6 in high, on which he ran a 3½-ton geared engine built in 1861; the Neath Abbey ironworks showed at the 1862 International Exhibition a 6¾-ton 0–4–0 of 2 ft 8 in gauge; and the first locomotive for the internal 18 inch gauge tramway round the works at Crewe, Ramsbottom's 2½-ton *Tiny*, was also built in that year. However, it was certainly the Festiniog that demonstrated the commercial possibilities of the narrow gauge public railway.

Eighteen-sixty can be taken as a useful date to mark the beginning of the end of the age of wrought iron in railway mechanical engineering, and the start of the change to steel. It was a gradual process, each step full of implications; the first important change to steel was for driving-wheel tyres, which was nearly contemporary with the start of the change to steel rails. But these two steps between them gradually transformed the limits within which designers had to work. Maximum permissible axle loadings with wrought iron were determined not by the size or strength of the rail so much as by the actual nature of the metal, which began to be crushed into separate laminations. Axle loads had risen from 3 tons at Rainhill to about 6 tons by 1850: by 1864 certain foreign railways were allowing 9 or 10 tons, but 8½-ton loads were the greatest in Britain. When this is compared with the 20–25 tons that had been reached by 1900, with the last generation of single-wheel express locomotives on the Midland, Great Northern, Great Central, and Great Western railways, the immense new scope that the new material gave is evident. Steel also solved some of those other headaches which had plagued locomotive men. Reliable crank axles could be made in steel, either as large single forgings or built up out of separate parts; driving wheels could then be braked; fast running with coupled wheels became possible; and so on.

The demand for increased power, which had enforced the change to the six-wheeled engine during the 1840s, was now leading to the development of the eight-wheeled machine. In Britain at any rate, the day of the locomotive with eight coupled wheels was not quite yet: the very first ones, some 0–8–0Ts for the Vale of Neath in 1864 and the Great Northern in 1866, had indeed appeared, but they were not followed up until the Barry Railway placed its outside-cylinder 0–8–0 tender engines in service in 1889, and these had originally been intended for Sweden. But the 4–4–0, which for well over half a century was the typical British passenger engine just as the 0–6–0 was the typical machine for freight, was beginning to appear in its final form, with a proper leading bogie.

There had been 4–4–0s earlier than 1860, and there had been engines with leading bogies. The first 4–4–0 tender engines were some by Gooch for the broad gauge South Wales Railway in 1855, but these were, like his *Iron Dukes*, strictly rigid-framed, and you could get away with that sort of inflexibility better on the broad than the standard gauge. There were several sorts of bogie 4–4–0T, from Gooch's of 1849 to some for the North London in 1855 and others. There was also Sturrock's one and only GNR 4–2–2 of 1853, which had a bogie. But all these engines were defective as vehicles. One might have thought that designers could have learnt something from America, where the bogie 4–4–0 had been the standard form of motive power since the late 1840s, that it was no good having an eight-wheeled vehicle with four wheels set rigidly in a frame and the other four rotating round a fixed pivot; the arrangement was geometrically unsound, since the wheels could not follow a circular track. What was needed was a pivot with side-play; and that side-play had to be controlled by springs, or else the guidance of the locomotive round curves would effectively be by the leading driving wheels, half-way along its length, and it would nose badly. But the fixed pivot was universal in British practice until 1863. Most engineers mistrusted the bogie, fearing that it would tend to derail and set itself across the track; and of course the short-wheelbase, fixed-pivot type they (but not the Americans) had in mind would tend to do just that.

The first British 4–4–0s to have a leading bogie of good length and with sideplay were some tank engines by William Adams, for the North London Railway in 1863. At first no springs were provided to control the lateral movement of the pivot, but very rapidly some rubber pads were fitted for this purpose. (It might be added here that rubber springing for locomotive purposes became quite popular during the 1850s, but its use declined thereafter and it was rare by 1880, although it has found a permanent place in rolling stock design.) The first tender engines with sound leading bogies on the same lines were built in 1865 by Cowan for the Great North of Scotland. This little line never had any 2–4–0s thereafter, and the message spread south from Aberdeen. Meanwhile, a number of fixed pivot 4–4–0s were turned out during the early 1860s, including the famous Stephenson outside cylinder engines for the Stockton & Darlington's extension into Lancashire, and some little inside cylinder ones for the Whitby & Pickering branch of the North Eastern. Like the GNS engines, the two first S & D 4–4–0s had full cabs on the American pattern, giving proper shelter to the crew; but these were almost as slow to spread as the bogie. It was said that the men did not like them: that they would sooner face the winter wind than be coddled in a cab. Maybe; it sounds an odd story nowadays, but then one thinks of the analogy of the open sports car.

As well as the bogie, there were various methods of allowing a certain amount of sideplay to a single pair of carrying wheels during the 1860s, either by using radial axles on W. B. Adams's pattern, or a Bissel truck. The former involved using axleboxes with curved sides running in curved horns which allowed them sideplay; all the curves were drawn from one focal point generally somewhere short of the nearest coupled axle. In the latter, the wheels were carried in a separate subframe which pivoted about a similar point, enabling the wheels to move in an identical lateral and radial path. Both types of movement were later developed; the Bissel or pony truck in one form or another was eventually favoured more because of the greater ease of providing it with side control, either by inclined plane or springing.

Two small but useful inventions were made in 1859 and are worth recording. One was the screw reverse, developed by John Ramsbottom of the L & NWR. There tends to be a fairly considerable force applied through the linkage to the reversing lever when an engine is moving with steam on; this is caused by the reaction due to leverage in the link and the fairly heavy friction of a slide valve forced down on to its working surface by steam pressure. This means that the driver, on some engines, moves the reversing lever *en route* at his peril. Right at the end of the steam era, this characteristic was still very noticeable with the various GWR pannier 0–6–0Ts, which had slide valves and reversing levers with Stephenson gear; they would start away from a station in full gear, and as soon as they were fairly under way the driver would shut off steam for a moment in order to shorten the cut-off without breaking his arm. If the control of the reverse was by a screw turned by a wheel, this danger was obviated and the cut-off could be altered without shutting off steam. Although there were designs of screw reverse which had a quick release catch, most had the drawback that reversing the locomotive meant a great many turns of the wheel, which was impractical for shunting; engines which had to do much of this therefore tended to retain the reversing lever.

The other invention was made by a Frenchman, Henri Giffard, who was not a railway engineer at all but an aeronaut. He had built a steam airship in 1852, and was now seeking to build a steam aeroplane. The trouble was the very low power-to-weight ratio of the steam engine, and in trying to improve this, and in particular to get rid of the feedwater pump, he devised the injector. This is a neat apparatus which appears to work in defiance of all natural laws, since it uses steam at *N* pounds per square inch to force water into a a boiler also at *N* pounds per square inch, and has no moving parts. In fact, it will still work even if steam is fed to it somewhat below the pressure in the boiler. Its action depends on impetus. A jet of steam moving at high speed is forced through a coned nozzle into the centre of a column of water, and although it condenses at once it imparts its velocity to the water, which emerges from another nozzle at almost as high a speed. This water jet is directed into an expanding cone, where it slows down but is still forced forward strongly enough to pass through the feedpipe and clack valve into the boiler. Although there was some trouble at first with adapting the injector to railway use, since a jolt would often disturb the accuracy of the jet and so cause it to stop working, the cones were adapted to allow for this and so the device became simple to use and maintain and quite dependable. Very rapidly it swept all the impediment of feed pumps away, and with them the necessity (since most of them were driven off a crosshead) to allow an engine to move—somewhere, anywhere—in order to pump water into its boiler. In later years the feed pump made a temporary reappearance; since an injector will not work where the feed water is too hot to condense sufficient steam, pumps had to be used in connection with feedwater heaters which (although they had been used on the Stockton & Darlington) were further experimented with during the twentieth century, though with more success elsewhere than in Britain.

One should not close an account of early locomotive practice without some mention of the part that private locomotive building firms played, particularly during the nineteenth century, in building up a highly important and nationally lucrative export business. The first and for the whole of this period most important firm was Robert Stephenson & Co., but it had important rivals even before 1860. Even though, like many continental railways, the larger companies in Britain preferred for commercial reasons to build their own locomotives and rolling stock, there was enough demand from the smaller lines and above all from railways outside Europe and America to keep the factories and drawing offices profitably employed, and in many respects the private builders' designs were often more advanced. They had to be; there was soon to be strong competition from other countries, particularly America. But for many years after 1860 Britain still retained the lead in the locomotive export trade.

There was, however, considerable argument (which is still heard) on the question of whether railways were well advised to manufacture their own machinery instead of buying it in from outside specialists. The matter was debated in the Institution of Civil Engineers in 1852. Joseph Locke and Mark Huish of the L & NWR were almost alone in supporting recent extensions to the railway workshops, particularly at Crewe. Locke pointed out that a large establishment was needed anyhow to maintain locomotives, which it was found could also build them, and more cheaply, amongst other reasons because parts of old machines could be reused, and because the men with knowledge of repair problems could guard against them in new construction. Huish claimed that the L & NWR had

had to build a rolling-mill of its own since the quality of rails obtained by competitive tender was not good enough. Brunel sat on the fence, supporting Locke but disagreeing with Huish. All others present, including Robert Stephenson, disagreed, and felt that manufacture was best left to specialists as a rule. The issue is not settled yet. Perhaps the weakness in Locke's case is that the men of (for instance) Crewe thus became judges in their own cause, never the best way to discover truth, as the last years of the Webb regime showed.

CHAPTER SEVEN

Other Forms of Motive Power

The rule of the steam locomotive over the world's railways may have been absolute during the nineteenth century, but it was not quite unchallenged. We have seen how it defeated the system of rope haulage by fixed engines during the 1830s; during the 1840s there was another assault launched by those who thought that fixed engines, with their lower-stressed working and higher thermal efficiency, promised better results than engines which had to move themselves as well as their payload. This time, however, the rope of hemp was replaced by, to use Robert Stephenson's phrase, a 'rope of air'.

The idea of using the pressure of the atmosphere, working against a vacuum, to propel a vehicle, had been ventilated somewhat earlier. In 1826 J. Vallance had built an experimental line 150 feet long in a shed at Brighton, on which ran a trolley with a body whose sides brushed lightly on all sides against the walls of a canvas tube through which the track ran. When the air was pumped out of the tube ahead of the car, it was forced slowly forward. However, there was an obvious difficulty about convincing entrepreneurs that canvas (or other) airtight tubes large enough to contain coaches and wagons should be built from one end of the country to another, and this caused the thoughts of several inventors to turn to a system in which a small tube, between the rails or along the side of the road, would be used; a piston would be drawn along this pipe by vacuum, and haul a train (or a road vehicle) along with it. The complication here was to provide a continuous airtight valve along which could pass the arm linking piston with hauled load. Several designs were proposed. One, by Henry Pinkus, had two strips of spring metal forced together above the slot in the pipe. Another, due to the brothers Jacob and Joseph Samuda, consisted basically of a hinged flap over the top of the slot, capable of being lifted by the arm as it passed, and held shut by gravity as well as vacuum.

16 The Liverpool and Manchester line where it passed under the older St Helens and Runcorn Gap, with a Rocket-type engine below and a Novelty-type one above

17 The 'Hibernia', built for the Dublin and Kingstown Railway in 1834 by Sharp, Roberts & Co.

18 The Leicester and Swannington's 0–6–0 'Atlas' of 1834, a development o
the Patentee type demonstrating how far locomotive design had come in th
five years since Rainhill

19 One of the Norris 4–2–0s of the Birmingham and Gloucester; a detail fron
Dolby's plate showing a trial run up the Lickey Incline in June 1840

0 A Crampton type 4–2–0, built for the Maryport and Carlisle Railway; from watercolour by E. W. Twining

1 McConnell's 'Bloomer' class 2–2–2, the mainstay of L & NW express orking in the late 1850s and 1860s (though not for long in this cabless state)

22 (*Above*) The L & NWR's Long-Boilered 'Trafalgar' drawn in 1849.
23 (*Below*) Alexander (Allan's 'Crewe-Type' 2–2–2; the 'Velocipede' of 1847

24 (*Below*) The Stockton and Darlington's 4–4–0 'Keswick', built by Robe
Stephenson & Co. in 1862

25 A typical coal wagon as used on early colliery tramways

26 A sprung flat wagon, Liverpool and Manchester railway 1830

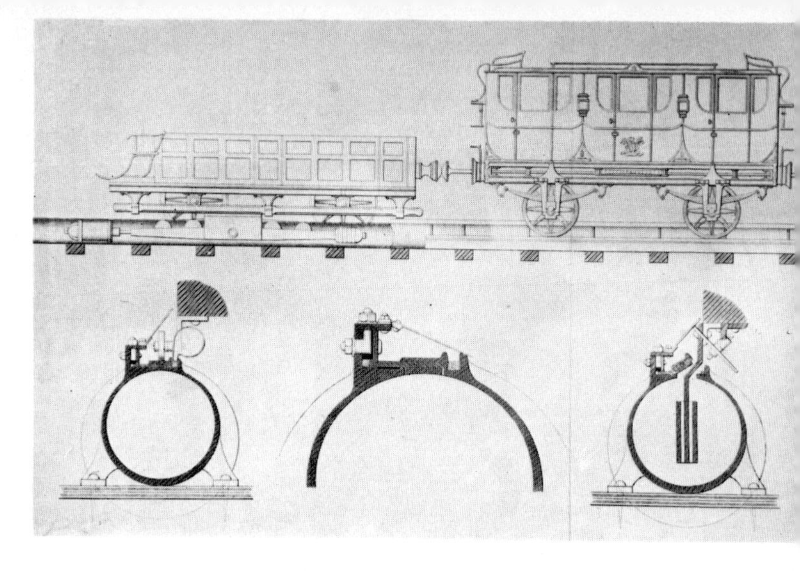

27 A section of an atmospheric train, with a coach drawn by a piston wag
showing the arrangement of a balanced piston travelling in the pipe ahead

28 The Minories terminus of the London and Blackwall Railway in 18
during the years of cable working. Note the early telegraph instrument on
extreme left

econd class coach of 1830, of the Liverpool and Manchester railway. It is open
ʼe the waist, in its original state with dumb buffers and a crude lever brake.
ıng buffers and couplings and screw brakes were fitted after the first few years

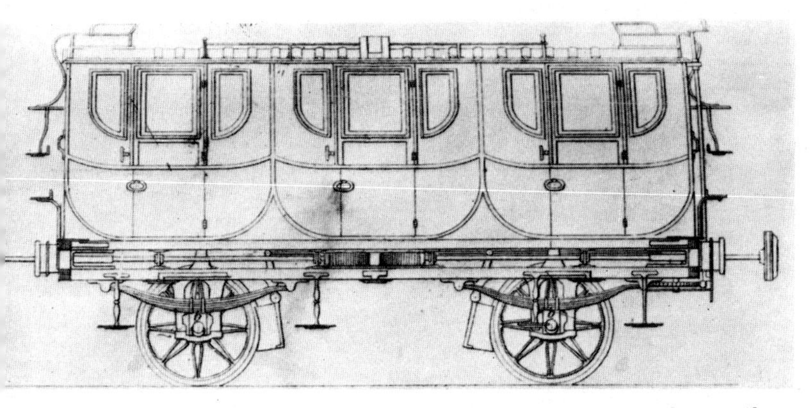

Above) First class coach of the 1840s, of the London and Birmingham railway.

Below) First class coach of the 1840s, of the Birmingham and Gloucester railway

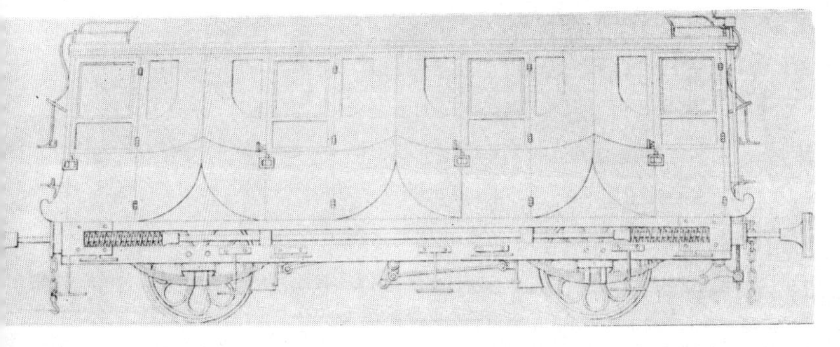

32 (*Above*) A junction signalbox of the 1850s, showing the separate posts each carrying semaphores for both directions on either line

33 (*Below*) A small country signalbox of the 1850s; the signalman surveys all his responsibilities

It was the Samudas, together with Samuel Clegg, who were responsible for all three of the public 'atmospheric' railways built in the British Isles. They started with a short, half-mile demonstration line, on an uncompleted section of the Birmingham, Bristol & Thames Junction Railway in west London, from the GWR main line by Wormwood Scrubbs to near the Uxbridge Road. A tube 9 inches in diameter was laid between the rails, exhausted by a 16 hp pump; and between June 1840 and early 1843, when the equipment was removed, it gave a series of public exhibitions and performances for the benefit of visiting engineers. Some of these were impressed, others doubtful. The device had previously been shown to work to admiration in a laboratory; now it was working in the open air, so probably (according to some) or possibly (according to others) it could be made to work in commercial service. But the acid question, 'could it be made to pay?' would not be answered without some railway trying it and seeing.

The first public atmospheric railway was in Ireland; a 1¾-mile extension, along the course of an old tramroad, of the Dublin & Kingstown line from Kingstown (now Dun Laoghaire) to Dalkey. The track rose throughout, at an average grade of 1 in 138 but with some lengths about 1 in 60; trains were therefore drawn uphill by a pumping station at Dalkey, and returned to Kingstown by gravity. The tube was 15 inches in diameter; as on all the other lines, the piston was carried on a special light four-wheeled vehicle which also carried the brakes, and there was provision for swinging the piston clear of the pipe on the downhill run. The normal degree of vacuum was 15 or 16 inches, which sufficed to haul a train of 66 tons (about ten or eleven four-wheeled coaches) up the hill at an average of 7½ mph, or lighter loads faster; on one occasion when the piston carriage had not been coupled to its train it set off inadvertently and is said to have reached a speed of 80 mph, which would certainly have been the land speed record of those days. When necessary, the vacuum could be increased to a maximum of about 27½ inches.

The Dalkey line was opened to the public, worked by atmospheric power, in March 1844. Barring occasional troubles, when a locomotive took over in substitution, it ran quite successfully until April 1854, when the line was closed, not through any failure, but to allow its gauge to be converted from 4 ft 8½ in to 5 ft 3 in before it was extended from Dalkey to Bray and a junction with the rest of the

Irish network. So it was reasonably successful. On the other hand, it did not really prove the commercial feasibility of the system. P. W. Barlow carried out a series of experiments during 1845, comparing the Dalkey line, where a 100-hp engine hauled 66 tons up 1 in 138 at 7½ mph, rather unfavourably with the cable-worked Tylers Hill incline on the Canterbury and Whitstable, where a 25-hp engine drew 35 tons up 1 in 48 at the same speed. The power loss on the Dalkey line was therefore 80 per cent, while it was only 40 per cent with the rope. However, it was felt that perhaps the equipment could be improved; certainly the public delighted in the smooth, silent, smokeless travel that the atmospheric system provided, and the idea caught the general imagination. Atmospheric railways were projected in every part of England; their supporters claimed that since the heavy weight of the locomotive need no longer be carried about, railways could now be built with lighter bridges and track, and steeper grades.

In fact, however, the Dalkey atmospheric line had almost everything in its favour, and the weaknesses of the system were less evident than on the other two railways that were actually worked by it. The fact that in one direction trains ran by gravity halved the wear and tear on the longitudinal valve; because the line was in a sheltered cutting throughout, the leather of the valve (no other material both flexible and airtight being available) was not much affected by the frost which on other lines caused it to dry out and crack; because there was only one train and one pumping station, the complications of pointwork, trains passing on the single line, altered plans due to late running, and telegraphing all this information to the various enginemen so that they could pump out the correct length at the right time (and to exhaust the pipe on a length of line took five minutes), were all minimized. The other British atmospheric lines were affected by all these difficulties, and were failures.

The first was a section of the London & Croydon railway, five miles in length from Croydon to Forest Hill, opened in January 1846. This was a single line, intended for local suburban traffic, running beside the double main line from London Bridge to Brighton and Dover. It was fitted with a 15 inch tube, which worked reasonably well on this more or less level section, though there were countless troubles of detail and several serious failures in the stationary pumping engines. However, there was a sign of trouble in the difficulty trains sometimes had in climbing the gradient over the flyover bridge which carried the track over the main line near Croydon; and when in February 1847 the line was extended for 2½ miles towards London, from Forest Hill to New Cross, trains were faced with the long 1 in 100 New Cross incline and their troubles were compounded. The 15 inch tube simply did not provide enough power; and the other mechanical difficulties simply reinforced the directors' doubts. Quite suddenly, in May 1847, they decided that the half-million that they had spent on the atmospheric system was bad money, and that they were not going to throw any good money after it. At short notice, and regardless of the inventors' protests, atmospheric working was abandoned and the equipment scrapped.

The other British atmospheric line, and the longest ever operated on the principle, was the twenty-mile section of the South Devon from Exeter to Newton Abbot. This broad gauge single line had been opened some time earlier, and Brunel did not hasten to instal the atmospheric equipment; while the first trains were worked by locomotives, he pointed out that the Croydon company was kindly developing the system on their behalf and sparing the South Devon shareholders the expense. However, when the Croydon line abandoned atmospheric working, the first section of the South Devon's, from Exeter to Teignmouth, was still not ready for public use, and the first atmospheric trains for passengers did not run until that September. They were extended to Newton in December 1847, and in the following months they gradually took over the whole of the working, banishing locomotives completely from the line, except in emergency. There were teething troubles, some of them well publicized, but the technique of operating the line was being mastered. The 18 inch pipe provided sufficient power for reasonably heavy trains on this level section, and the public were charmed by the clean, silent, and speedy travel. A 25 inch pipe was being installed on the next section, over the hill past Dainton to Totnes, with its 1 in 42 grades, for Brunel was taking the claims of the atmospheric protagonists at face value and (as Bryan Morgan points out in his companion book) sharpening the grades of the line over the southern outliers of Dartmoor. It was intended to fit an expanding piston to the haulage car, to allow through working past Newton Abbot. Yet in September 1848 the South Devon, like the Croydon, abandoned atmospheric working, though in this case not so precipitately, and reverted to locomotives while writing off the enormous investment in fixed plant that the atmospheric experiment had represented. In this case the trouble was with the continuous valve; the leather was rotting and the cast iron of the pipe corroding due to a chemical action encouraged probably by the salt from the sea nearby. A new type of valve was being experimented with, but the company was faced with the enormous expense of renewing the old valve, with no guarantee that the trouble would not recur, and they had had sufficient experience of operating the line to discover that, however much the public might approve of atmospheric working, the promised economy in fuel and engine power was simply not being obtained. It was not for some years that the equipment was removed, as Brunel continued to have hopes of eventual success; but it lay idle after that September, with only a year of commercial operation to its credit.

Only one other public atmospheric railway ever operated; a 2-kilometre line in the suburbs of Paris, from Bois de Vecinet to St Germain. This was opened in April 1847, and continued successfully until July 1860. But it was another Dalkey operation, only a more powerful one, with a 25 inch pipe and a 1 in 29 grade; so it worked under the same favourable circumstances. Robert Stephenson and the other critics turned out to be right; the atmospheric system perhaps had a place in a small way for short and special lines, but it was quite unsuited and too inflexible for main line working.

Oddly enough, nobody seems to have thought of powering trains not by vacuum but by compressed air, which by using higher pressure could have allowed much greater power to be obtained out of a smaller pipe (although the problem of leakage would have been correspondingly worse). J. G. Shuttleworth in 1842 published a scheme for hydraulic propulsion on somewhat similar principles, with waterpressure in the pipe behind the piston. The difficulty about this proposal was that a great deal of power would be needed to force large amounts of water through the pipe at the same speed as the train; Shuttleworth proposed therefore that the sections of pipe under hydraulic pressure should be only 92 yards long, with 150-yard sections of 'skeleton' pipe between serving to align the piston through the necessary valves. Trains would thus have progressed in a series of grasshopper leaps. Shuttleworth pointed out that in mountain country sufficient hydraulic power was available naturally and no pumping stations would be needed (Samuda had also made the same claim for the atmospheric system, as a vacuum could be obtained by allowing water to run out of a sealed tank). But almost needless to say, no hydraulically propelled line was ever built.

The essential question in the locomotive versus atmospheric system debate was whether it was more economical that the power to haul a train be generated on the train itself, or at the lineside. The issue remains a live one to this day, though now the method by which stationary power sources transmit the necessary energy is by electricity. This is a very much more efficient means of transmission than either rope or vacuum; losses are very small, and the practical distance is very great, so that there is now no need for generating stations every couple of miles, while the actual application of power remains under the control of the driver of the train, and not the remote engineman. The first electric railways, however, fall outside the period covered in this book, since it was not until Werner von Siemens's experiments of 1879 and Thomas Edison's of 1880 that sufficiently powerful and reliable electric motors and generators began to be made. The first two electrically powered railways in Britain both date from 1883; Magnus Volk's line along the beach at Brighton (which still runs) and the Portrush & Giant's Causeway in Ulster. Electricity was first thought of as a cheap power suited to propel light loads on tramways feeding into steam main lines, and it was not until later that the main line electric railway was put forward. The nation which led in early electric traction was certainly America, where fifty lines were in operation at the end of 1888 (while only seven existed in Britain), and which had the first main line electrification (Baltimore & Ohio, seven miles through Baltimore, 1894/5). Oddly enough the very first vehicle to move on rails under electric power was much earlier, and in Scotland; R. Davidson, in 1842, experimented with a 7 ton four-wheeled battery-powered locomotive on the Edinburgh & Glasgow line. It was able to move 6 tons at 4 mph, but no more, so nothing then came of it.

With the atmospheric challenge disposed of, the steam locomotive had nearly half a century of unquestioned practical predominance before its next rival had to be taken seriously.

CHAPTER EIGHT

Carriage and Wagon Development to 1860

Wagons used on tramways, naturally enough, bore a considerable resemblance to the horse-drawn carts they replaced; relatively light wooden bodies built on a frame contained between the wheels and little longer than the wheelbase. The main difference was that there was no need to make provision for the front axle to swivel, and in consequence of this the shafts and traces for the horse were also simpler, as the animal did not have to pull in any other direction than straight forwards. On many lines one horse could readily draw several wagons, and so means had to be provided to couple them together; this was generally by a single link secured at each end by a pin held in the jaws of a plain bracket fastened to the end of the frame of each wagon. Since most tramways carried coal or other minerals and little else, the majority of wagons were made with bodies whose sides tapered in towards the floor, where a trapdoor allowed rapid discharge between the rails, often enough directly into the hold of a ship.

The first locomotive-hauled wagons were of this kind. But as railways spread, general freight became more important than it had been, and the variety of bodies designed to cope with different sorts of traffic therefore increased. The size of wagons also increased, though much more slowly; a locomotive could haul a much larger load than a horse, but in most stations wagons still had to be man-handled or horse-shunted to and from the loading platforms, and to make up a train, using the numerous small turntables and light tracks crossing the main ones at right-angles that are conspicuous in many pictures of early railway yards. For this reason, it was long thought impractical to increase wagon sizes very much, and it was not until the 1840s and 1850s that it was at all common to find locomotives being used for shunting. Another change that was soon found necessary was in the construction of the frame. The link-and-pin coupling, attached to the centre of the crosspiece joining the ends of the two main longitudinal frame timbers, was adequate for locomotive haulage in itself, and indeed has remained in use until now on some industrial lines; but with increased train loads it was found that the impacts of wagons butting into each other could be sustained with less damage if the rigid central link was replaced by a loose chain coupling, and the two side frame members were extended so that they formed buffers, able to butt against the corresponding part of the next wagon.

A typical coal wagon of this kind is illustrated in plate 25, taken from the 1838 edition of Wood's *Treatise*. Coupling hooks, side-frames lying between the wheels and extended into buffers, and hopper-shaped body are all clear. There were no springs, and the axles were carried in plain bearings; that part of the wagon floor which was between the axles was hinged and could be let down by releasing a catch; and the handbrake was of a very simple kind, acting on two wheels but fitted on one side of the wagon only. The example illustrated was just over nine feet long, and carried about 2½ tons.

This sort of vehicle did perfectly well for the short, slow run from a colliery to the nearest water. But being unsprung it was not suitable for speeds of more than 10–12 mph, and the lubrication of its plain bearings would soon give trouble if it kept rolling at this pace for very long, since this was no more than an occasional smear of grease poked through the wheels by a boy with a long stick. For the first main lines something much better was soon found to be needed, and one of the early Liverpool & Manchester wagons is illustrated in plate 26, from the same source. Intended for general freight, this was, like most of the line's first wagons, a simple platform on wheels; but it was rather larger than the older coal wagon, being some 12 ft long and 7 ft wide. It was also very much more strongly built, with frames inside and outside the wheels, and all four longitudinals extended to form buffers; the floor was carried above the frame, and clear of the wheels, on cross-timbers. The bearings were outside the wheels, the handbrake acted on one pair of wheels only (but on both of them), and for the first time the wheels were sprung, with the axleboxes running in horns and the weight carried by pins to overhung laminated springs. The wagon could be converted from a flat to a low-sided one by fitting portable sides and ends, secured by means of pins falling into holes in the floor. These wagons, and their successors, could carry up to 3½ tons. Some were given bodies to fit them for carrying livestock, though flat and open trucks were also used for this purpose. Drovers, shepherds, and swineherds accompanied their trains in some numbers, but there were still a lot of cases of animals jumping out, sometimes causing derailments when they were run over.

In service, this type of wagon revealed a number of shortcomings. The first of these was that it offered the freight very little protection from damage. Much of the stuff carried, especially in the textile manufacturing district served, was easily spoiled by water and had to be protected from the weather. The only means of protection was by means of tarpaulins lashed down over the tops. Tarpaulins had been used on canals to keep goods dry, and served this purpose on railways reasonably well (though water tended to accumulate in the folds and a gang of twenty men had to be maintained halfway along the line in wet weather in order to remove it from passing wagons); but since they had been soaked in tar to make them weatherproof they were rather inflammable, and in their new environment, enlivened with showers of sparks and hot coals from the engine, a new problem thus arose. Still, often enough the tarpaulin was less easily lit than the goods it covered.

The other series of shortcomings arose from the design of the vehicle. It was a very considerable improvement on what had gone before, but still not adequate for main line work. In particular, the continued use of solid buffers formed out of extensions of the frame longitudinals was objectionable at the speeds of trains on the L & M; some pretty considerable impacts occurred if the brakes were put on sharply, just as some rather violent snatches were felt as the couplings tightened on starting. Passengers were the first to complain, and were given sprung buffers and couplings very early; but though freight was dumb, the toll of damage claims and the bills for repairs to wagons soon proved that buffing and drawgear needed springs on all vehicles, and that the fairly heavy cost was money well spent. Some experimentation took place to find out how the springs were best applied, but the commonest arrangement (and one still met with today) was some version of that illustrated below. This particular layout is unusual in that it uses four laminated springs; two were commoner, and they were more often placed at the ends of the vehicle than in the middle, but the principle is well shown. The buffers force back the outer ends of the spring, and the coupling draws the centre forward. The drawbar linking the couplings is continuous from one end to the other, not being affected by spring action; but starting and stopping forces are transmitted to the wagon through the springs, through their being forced back onto one central stop by the buffers or drawn forward onto two stops at the sides by the coupling. Laminated springs, being made of steel by craftsmen, were still quite expensive, and several systems (including that first used on the L & M) were devised to enable one spring only to be used per vehicle; but since these involved the use of cranks and levers there were some fairly considerable maintenance complications and the idea was discarded.

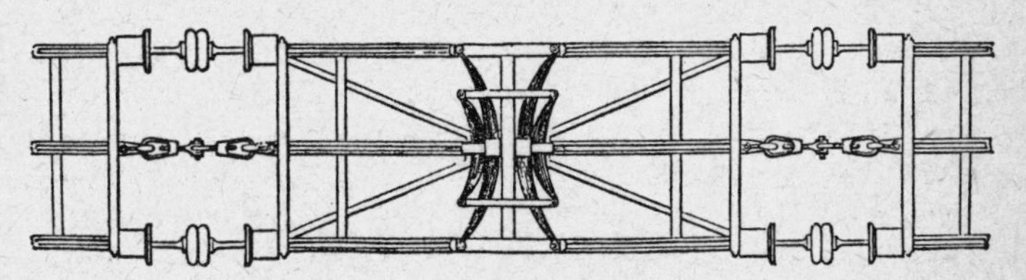

Figure 7 Detail of coach underframe, showing the use of laminated springs in buffing and drawgear and also screw couplings

Since fig. 7 also shows a screw coupling, we shall mention it here although the device was never used on freight stock in Britain, but to this day remains standard on passenger stock. It was patented by Henry Booth of the Liverpool & Manchester in 1836. Until that time the solid chains used in couplings inevitably had to be loose (otherwise they could never be attached or removed from the hooks) and so jerking at every start was unavoidable. By using a linkage with a central rod, capable of being turned by a handle, with a left and a right hand thread at either end so that the links at each end could be drawn together, Booth made it possible to tighten the coupling quite readily so that the buffers could be brought into contact and even some pressure applied, and the whole train made to start smoothly as a single unit. This is the great advantage of the European buffer-and-coupling system, even though it is now obsolescent and will be replaced by one of the stronger patterns of central coupling already almost universal in the rest of the world; each one of these, being a solid connection, inevitably has some slack between buffing and drawing faces.

Little more need be said about freight stock before 1860, since changes were extremely slow. Covered vans, for instance, were only introduced in the late 1840s, even though (as Henry Henson, the patenter of a type of van with sliding roof to allow cranage, pointed out to the Institution of Mechanical Engineers in 1851) their advantages were large and obvious. There was freedom from damage by weather, and saving the considerable cost of tarpaulins; risk of physical damage was reduced and the freight could in any case not fall off completely, which happened quite often from flat trucks; and vans were lockable and harder to pilfer from. Iron frames also were unknown before the mid-1840s, though as W. A. Adams pointed out to the same body in 1852, they had considerable advantages. Wooden-framed wagons by then had a life expectation of some ten years, but iron frames would last a very long time, while they weighed less, needed much less maintenance, and cost very little more originally. By 1852 iron-framed wagons had been adopted as standard by the Midland, London & North Western, and Taff Vale railways, and most of the others soon followed. By that time the average wood-framed wagon carried 6 tons and weighed 3¼ tons; the average iron-framed one carried 6 and weighed 3.

Before passing to the subject of passenger vehicles a few words should be said about axleboxes, bearings, and lubrication. The plain inside bearing of the old chaldron wagons had had to be discarded with the introduction of springing, and replaced by an axlebox free to move up and down between two horns fixed in hornplates attached to the framing. The spring carried the weight by resting in some convenient manner, directly, or indirectly, on the axlebox. Inside this box the journal of the axle turned in a bearing, generally at this time made of brass. During the 1830s there was a prevalent belief (true up to a point) that the smaller the diameter of the journal, the less the friction. Wood illustrates an axlebox in which the desirable object of reducing friction was married to the even more desirable object of having a journal large enough to be strong, by reducing the latter's diameter in three steps towards the end of the axle. (This was a fairly complicated piece of fitting work, since it also needed a correspondingly stepped bearing. With improved lubrication experience showed it was unnecessary and the parallel journal returned unchallenged.)

Lubrication on British railways was until the mid-1840s entirely by grease. Several different sorts were used, but Nicholas Wood gives the recipe for the most popular: 'Take 3 lbs of tallow and 6 lbs of palm oil to each gallon of water containing ½-lb of washing soda. Simmer for some hours at about 200°F, do not allow to boil; then cool; the result should have the consistency of butter.' Yes, though judging by a sample of the product that remained in the stores of the Talyllyn Railway in 1951, butter on a cool day. The mixture was applied to the bearing by being stuffed into a reservoir (with a lid) at the top of the axlebox, but being a solid it would not melt and run down the channels provided to the bearing surface until the wheels were rolling and the bearing had started to run hot. Locomotive lubrication, it may be added, was on similar principles; with the exception that valves and cylinders could not well be reached by melting grease in this way. One common expedient adopted by enginemen to provide lubrication while running was therefore for the fireman to go out along the plating to the front of the engine with a ball of grease, and on the driver shutting off steam, to open the smokebox door and drop this pill down the blastpipe. The driver would then allow the engine to coast for a few moments, to allow time for the grease to melt and the healing fluid to run down the pipes to the valves.

Lubrication by oil was universal in America, and had been tried and discarded in early days on the Liverpool & Manchester. At first vegetable oil was used (olive oil from Lucca was recommended for expresses), but during the 1850s it began to be replaced by mineral oil. Oil lubrication was reintroduced to British railways by P. R. Hodge, one of McConnell's assistants at Wolverton works on the L & N W, about 1850. The Americans had evolved, and we copied, the now standard axlebox in which oil was retained beneath the axle by a mass of cotton waste, flax, sponge, or pads of other absorbent material stored in a reservoir at the bottom of the box and held in contact with the underside of the axle. Thus it was fed to the bearing more or less directly. This had the advantage that the bearing surface did not have to be reduced by holes and channels cut away to allow the grease to enter. At first it was felt that the oil would tend to leak away, and would have to be retained somehow, so the first L & N W boxes had a leather ring round the axle where it entered the box to prevent oil escaping. However, it was soon found that the leather remained dry, which proved it was not needed. The early L & N W boxes also had a second reservoir beneath that containing the cotton waste, with a channel leading up to one end of the bearing; the theory being that used oil would drip down this channel, to be removed from the reservoir at intervals through a drainplug. Again, this was found an unnecessary complication; little oil found its way through, and what did was clean and fit for re-use. After a while it was found that the simpler oil boxes then designed were cheaper to make than grease boxes, and the bill for lubricant was cut by 20 per cent. By 1860 grease lubrication was well on the way out.

Passenger-carrying rail vehicles were not unknown during the tramway age; possibly the first was on the Swansea & Oystermouth railway, which was opened in 1807 and on which a horse-drawn passenger service seems to have been started, without any particular legal authority, very soon after. The first passengers to be hauled (officially) by locomotives were on the Stockton & Darlington. For the opening ceremony on 27 September 1825 it was realized rather late that the directors and several important local personalities would want to ride on the train, and it would hardly do to have them hopping about among the coals. In some haste, therefore, a local coachbuilder was commissioned to run up a coach body on a wagon underframe. This coach, called the *Experiment*, was part of the inaugural train. It is not quite certain what kind of a vehicle it was; the only description of it that we have dating from that year is in the coachmaker's bill, in the not unreasonable sum of £80, for 'one coach body put up with door at each end, glass panes to the windows, a table and seats for inside, top seat and steps, cushioned and carpeted'. So it was evidently fairly comfortable. Seizing on the words 'door at each end', the bold Colonel Pangborn (US Army), organizer of the railroad section of the World's Columbian Exposition at St Louis, Missouri, in 1892, constructed and had illustrated a vehicle rather like a henhouse on wheels, which had a door at each end and windows all right, and looked as if it might have been the primeval ancestor of all transatlantic coaches, but whose connection with the Stockton & Darlington is probably strictly apocryphal, though even some British authorities have assumed it. Certainly a scheduled passenger service was later operated on the S & D by a horse-coach, named *Experiment*, which was in essence an ordinary road stage coach mounted on a wagon frame, sprung by, suspension from C-springs through leather straps, exactly following road practice.

The Liverpool & Manchester, which expected to earn a great deal of its revenue from passenger traffic, did rather better, and its first passenger stock was influenced by, but not a copy of, road coaches. There were a number of more or less experimental oddities, like the eight-wheeled grandstand 24 feet long which carried the band on opening day, but most of the passenger stock was reasonably standard; all four-wheeled, mounted on sprung frames not unlike those already described for the goods stock, and on a seven-foot wheelbase. Buffers were formed by extensions of the frame pieces at first, though on the first-class coaches they were padded with horsehair stuffing; but by about 1835 sprung buffers had replaced all these. The bodies of the first-class coaches consisted of three compartments built together, each about seven feet square, with luggage and brakesmen (but no passengers) riding on the roof. Second class passengers had similar accommodation, but hard seats, and although there was a roof the sides were not carried up above waist level. Third class customers had open trucks and little enough to sit on.

These early Liverpool & Manchester coaches served as models for the next thirty or forty years, although of course many improvements were made, and just as many experiments. The buffing and coupling system worked out on the L & M was taken as a standard, although there was some diversity elsewhere for a while; two lines, the Dublin & Kingstown (1834) and the Newcastle & Carlisle (1835) used a single central buffer, acting on a strong coil spring, with separate hook-and-chain couplings; these were persevered with for some time, but did not spread since most people felt that the single centre buffer was unstable while vehicles were being propelled, and eventually it was done away with for the sake of conformity.

These were, incidentally, possibly the first examples of the use of coil springs in heavy engineering; and before long they were used to some extent instead of laminated springs in buffers and drawgear. They also became moderately popular in suspensions, both carriage and locomotive, though they were always extremely rare in these applications outside Britain. One reason for this is that, while the motion of a laminated spring is considerably restrained by friction between its plates, so that on being released from compression it returns to its original form and stays there, the coil spring gives out again very nearly all the energy used to compress it, and will bounce. In suspensions this will be damped by other parts, but even so the tendency remains; and large steel (or iron) viaducts, fairly rare in Britain but much commoner abroad, are also resilient, springy structures with a tendency to vibrate. Thus a vehicle with coil springs crossing such a bridge at a speed when the two periods of vibration correspond will find itself doing unexpected and alarming things; hence the speed limits on most British steel viaducts.

The third principal form of spring, the volute spring, made out of plate cut into a tapered strip, stood on edge and coiled into a spiral, has found little use in carriage and wagon suspensions (though much more in locomotives); it was patented in Austria in 1848. Since the plate is coiled fairly tightly, there is a certain amount of internal friction in this variety of spring. It is nowadays the normal type of buffer spring. Rubber springing has also found a place in railway work since George Spencer's original patents in the 1840s.

None of the original L & M coaches survive; some replicas of them were built by the L M S for the centenary of the railway in 1930, to be hauled by the original L & M 0–4–2 *Lion* (which does survive, and is operable), but they incorporate certain post-1830 improvements, such as sprung buffers and couplings. Perhaps the earliest coaches which survived long enough to be photographed were a few on the Bodmin & Wadebridge (1834), which remote and isolated Cornish outpost remained in more or less its original state until the 1890s. These were considerably cruder and smaller vehicles; the two-compartment second now in the York museum noticeably so, though the line also had some three-compartment coaches. Bryan Morgan's *Railway Relics* lists these and other survivors.

By 1840 and for a quarter of a century thereafter, the typical passenger coach was a three-compartment four-wheeler. In one respect the first L & M coaches were proved defective; in order to minimize the encroachment of the wheel arches into the passenger space, the wheels were so placed that they came directly underneath the divisions between the compartments. This gave what was found to be an inconveniently short wheelbase, leading to rough riding and pitching, and so the wheelbase had to be increased beyond one-third of the coach length. There were two conflicting considerations here. In order to minimize friction, it was felt wise to have coach wheels as large as possible; yet in order to keep the centre of gravity down it was desired to have the floor of the coach as low as possible. Yet if the wheels came up above floor level, the wheel arches had to be accommodated beneath the seats, since otherwise passengers would inevitably trip over them. Plates 30 and 31 give two examples of the way this difficulty was faced in the 1840s. The London & Birmingham first illustrated in plate 30 was a less ambitious but much more typical vehicle, 20 feet long over buffers and 6 ft 6 in wide overall, seating eighteen passengers three-a-side (none too luxuriously) in three compartments. The nine-foot wheelbase placed the axles under the front edges of the seats, so relatively small wheels (3 ft diameter) had to be used so that they could be fitted beneath the floor. There was a seat for a brakesman at each end of the roof, and a screw brake (acting on all four wheels) for him to operate at one end only. Luggage was still carried on the roof (although the L & N W went over to using separate luggage vans on main-line trains about 1848, as simpler, faster, and safer) and roof rails and racks were therefore still provided.

The other vehicle, dating from several years later, is a much grander and less typical First from the Birmingham & Gloucester. It was 22 ft 6 in long over buffers and 7 ft 6 in wide over the body, so that its eighteen passengers had considerably more room. The wheels were about 3 ft 6 in diameter, but oddly enough the buffer and frame height shown in the drawing is some six inches lower than the London & Birmingham's (which became the standard) and so presumably these vehicles had either to be given bigger wheels or raised on their springs once the two lines had been linked in Birmingham (which happened almost at once). In any case, the wheel arches came through the floor quite considerably, and in order to accommodate the 11-foot wheelbase the compartments were re-arranged, with two normal ones placed centrally and two coupés at either end. They must therefore have been rather more expensive to build, which explains why they were untypical. Brakes and brakes-men's arrangements were similar to those on the L & B coach.

Various types of first class saloon coaches were tried by different lines at different times, to cater for private parties, family travel, and so on; those were the days when a compartment seating six was not likely to be large enough to contain most middle- and upper-class families and their retinues of servants. Saloons generally followed the arrangement of sofa-type seating round a central table, backs to the windows. But they were never very numerous.

The treatment of second class passengers varied from one railway to another. Their coaches were generally similar to firsts in outline, though definitely poor relations; most lines gave them walls and windows as well as seats and roofs. None gave any upholstery before 1850, and some felt that coaches open above the waist would do, and might encourage customers to pay up and go first. Third class travellers, of course, were something else again. In most cases, their early accommodation was spartan indeed; roofs and indeed seats were treated as optional, the only feature being regarded as desirable was a wall up to waist level to prevent the wretches falling out and getting under the wheels. However, the inhumanity of treating even third class passengers on the same footing as sheep or swine in bad weather was soon felt, and by the end of the 1830s some modest improvements of their lot had been made fairly generally. The process was carried on and made compulsory by the Regulation of Railways Act 1844, otherwise known as Gladstone's Act, which among other reforms insisted that each line of railway must be served at least once a day in each direction by a train conveying third class passengers, at a fare of one penny a mile and at a speed of not less than 12 mph including stoppages, in vehicles with seats and protected from the weather 'as far as consistent with the admission of light and air'.

The law was thus not by any means one which coddled or pampered. It still allowed certain variations on the cattle-truck theme; there had to be roofs, walls, and seats, but sliding shutters might still do for windows. Furthermore, the old coaches were not prohibited, and remained in service for some time, either on certain lines (notably in Scotland) as fourth class, or in excursion and special traffic. But in general the companies recognized the spirit of the law and went further than the letter told them. Best of all was the Midland, which was arguably the leader throughout the nineteenth century in the provision of passenger amenities, which by 1845 had a series of three-compartment four-wheeled thirds in service. These seated five a side; but they had doors, droplight windows, and even a lamp (which illuminated the whole coach since there were no partitions).

Of course in fine weather it was no doubt very pleasant to go for a spin down to Brighton or somewhere in an open third. Plenty of fresh air and sunshine, a panorama of natural beauty and bucolic activity, no doubt entertaining company, and who knows what entertaining alarums and excursions by the way?

> On the 29th of June, in the ½ past 5 o'clock train, shortly after leaving Greenock for Glasgow, a smell of burning was felt in one of the 3rd-class carriages, immediately thereafter the flames burst out in the dress of one of the females, and as the train was at a considerable speed, and the wind was high, the utmost consternation prevailed. By the presence of mind and the activity of a young seaman, the flames were extinguished, but not before the female's gown was consumed, all to the body and sleeves. The accident occurred from a red-hot cinder ejected from the funnel of the engine.

Very painful and embarrassing for the young lady no doubt, but the resourceful sailor may have had mixed feelings. Proceedings in a Parliamentary Car may have been more comfortable, and no doubt the difference could be a matter of life and death for the old and infirm in winter, but as always progress makes life duller.

Broad gauge coaches on the GWR were, in the 1840s, something of an advance. For one thing, they were practically all on six wheels; and the six-wheeled standard gauge coach remained something uncommon until the sixties. Not much advantage was taken of the potentialities of the increased loading gauge, but the typical early GWR coach was 24 feet long and 9 feet wide, and seating its first class customers four abreast gave them more room than the London & Birmingham (if not as much as the Birmingham & Gloucester). There were generally four first class compartments per coach, or six seconds, the latter packing them in six a side. The GWR did not do very much at all for its third class passengers until the Act, and the fatalities in the accident at Sonning in 1841 where deaths resulted from the lack of protection, forced their hands. (One might here remark that a spartan attitude to the third class was one of the less attractive and more enduring GWR traditions.)

Neither on broad nor standard gauges were passengers allowed much height; the stagecoach tradition (carried on still by all types of motorcar except the London taxi) was that passengers had to sit down and take their hats off. It was not until the first coaches of the Metropolitan Railway in 1863, where some compression could have been excused, that a six-foot man could stand up with his hat on in a train. This was no doubt partly because of the low-centre-of-gravity fetish, which had a powerful influence on passenger stock as well as locomotives. One extraordinary design to which it led was the Curtis frame, used by the London & Greenwich. With this, the frame was slung below the axles, and the body held up clear of the wheels by cross-members. One advantage that was claimed for the system was that in the case of derailment or of a broken axle, the coach would skate along on its frame, which would still guide it along the track; an argument that was felt to have some force on a line like the L & G, which ran all the way along a viaduct.

No provision was made for any lavatory or refreshment facility in coaches in the early days, except occasionally that some kind of commode would be fitted in specially luxurious vehicles designed for royalty. Everybody else had to get out of the train at certain stations, and make up their minds what their priorities were. The GWR had a contract with the lessee of the refreshment rooms at Swindon that all trains should stop there for twenty minutes, which was probably time enough; with the march of progress it came to be thought too long but a great lawsuit was needed to reduce it during the 1860s. Eating on trains came very much later, in the 1870s; but not so long after the first full set of sanitation in a coach, and both became available to the ordinary reasonably well-heeled passenger at about the same time. However, at first he had to take his meal at his seat. Corridors, and gangway connections between coaches to enable dining cars to be reached by all, came later still; the first all-gangway train did not appear until 1891, when the GWR put one into service. According to Hamilton Ellis, the first British coach with a complete lavatory was a four-wheeled invalid carriage built for the South Eastern in 1860; it was also the first with a proper bed, and had an end door to allow a stretcher to be carried in and out.

Some kind of sleeping accommodation had been provided much earlier, in fact right at the start of overnight passenger train operation, which commenced with the completion of the main line from London to Liverpool and Manchester in 1838. The Grand Junction and London & Birmingham companies each provided a combined Royal Mail and sleeping car; the mails carried in a chest on the roof under the eye of a guard, the sleepers recumbent horizontally in a compartment below, lying parallel to the rails, with their feet protruding into a boot which extended out at the end of the coach. A travelling Sorting Office for the mail was introduced at the same time, but the devices for picking up and dropping sacks of mail by the lineside in nets and chutes without slowing down came rather later, patented by John Ramsay in 1848. As compartments grew larger, it became feasible to instal stretchers or bed-sticks in any ordinary first, and this was generally done by private arrangement as required. The cushioned extensions by which the space between the seats can be made up to form one continuous divan, still met with for instance in first class in Spain and Germany, were never common in Britain, although Queen Adelaide's saloon on the London & Birmingham in 1842 had them.

Carriage lighting was completely absent at first; those who were not content to sit in the dark could purchase a small dark lantern, carrying a candle, which could be hooked into the upholstery above one's shoulder. These occasionally started fires. The alternative was for the railway to provide lamps itself, and this was eventually done, the GWR making a start with its first class in 1842. Oil lamps of one pattern or another, filled and lit at suitable stations, were placed in holes provided for them in coach roofs, and stopped with some kind of bung in the lamp's absence. Some ingenuity was displayed, especially in the lower classes, in ensuring that the lamp could be seen by, even if it could hardly be said to illuminate, as many passengers as possible. The first gas lamps were used on the Metropolitan, in 1863; this line's rolling stock was quite a remarkable advance in several ways. This first installation used coal gas, stored at low pressure in a rubber bag on the carriage roof; it needed to be recharged rather frequently. Some other lines, including the Lancashire & Yorkshire and North London, experimented soon after with a high-pressure gasholder in the guard's van and pipes along the train. The most satisfactory pattern of gas lighting (apart from the increased risk of fire following serious accidents) was the Pintsch oil-gas system, in which a liquefied supply sufficient for forty hours was stored in cylinders under each coach. Electric lighting began to be experimented with in the 1880s.

Carriage heating was a moderately difficult business, and at first the railways rather shied away from it; Queen Victoria's 1843 saloon on the London & Birmingham had steam heating provided by a small flash boiler, burning oil, carried on the coach together with an attendant, which showed what could be done even then when engineers put their minds to it; but it was quite impractical to go to these lengths for ordinary travellers, who had to make do as a rule with hot water bottles, supplied at the stations. The many-sided Mr Webb devised for the London & North Western a form of heating can that operated by slowly releasing the latent heat of fusion of sodium acetate, and could at least be encouraged to give out a few more calories by shaking it vigorously. And it was with these things that the British railway passenger had in general to put up with until steam heating supplied from the engine arrived with the twentieth century. Exceptions were Pullman cars after the 1870s, which, like Russian coaches then and now, had their own independent boilers and heating system.

As we have seen, the four-wheeled coach was still the normal thing until the sixties, when gradually the six-wheeler, with its better riding at speed and larger capacity, began to increase its numbers. By the 1880s the four-wheeler was definitely obsolete on main line work, though some examples survived on branches and in suburban traffic for many years after that. The first eight-wheeled coach was the GWR Royal Saloon of 1842, a splendiferous affair with a semaphore on the roof, so that the Queen could instruct the driver to go faster or (more usually) slower; they were followed by the *Long Charleys*, built for the commencement of the broad-gauge Birmingham service in 1852, which had three first- and four second-class compartments. Other eight-wheelers were on the Metropolitan and Great Northern railways, all for suburban traffic; one major motive for them here was that by abolishing half the gaps between the coaches they economized in train length and platform space. But all of them were strictly rigid, with all four axles solidly attached to the frames; no nonsense about bogies. W. B. Adams may have had a better idea when he built what he described as an eight-wheeled coach for the Eastern Counties in 1847, but which was really two separate four-wheelers very closely attached with a flexible connection. British railways were as suspicious of the carriage bogie as they had been of the locomotive bogie; the first bogie coach in Britain (and, for that matter, the first with a steel frame), was built for the Festiniog Railway in 1873 (and is still in service). Once this little two-foot gauge line had broken the ice, others followed, notably the Midland, which by 1875 had sixty-eight bogie coaches, including thirty-six Pullmans, and one twelve-wheeler. On the other hand, the Midland's Manager, James Allport, had just been on a tour of the United States, where he had seen something of the standards of comfort and amenity that were reached there, depending to quite a large extent on the extra length of body that the flexibility attainable with bogies allowed.

During the period covered by this book, railway carriage building was not taken very seriously, apart from a very few special vehicles and first class stock on the better lines. Most of the passenger equipment was basic and boxlike; the highwater mark of elegance, comfort, and workmanship in railway coach design was reached during the period between 1880 and 1914. Even a matter as important as brakes had not, by 1860, made very much progress. Brakesmen sitting on the roofs were still the regular thing. The Atkinson brake, tried in 1845, allowed the guard in his van to apply all the brakes on the train by means of a rope running under the carriages and wound tight on application by a drum on the axle of the van; so a crude form of power-assisted brake was known early. But the coupling up of the rope, or rather its threading along a marshalled train, was impracticably slow and difficult. A variant of this brake, using a chain, was introduced on the Midland by Clark and Wilkins during the 1860s, and again, modified by Webb, on the London & North Western. The Highland and Lancashire & Yorkshire used a throughout mechanical brake, with a continuous shaft linked by universal joints running beneath the train, turned by the guard's (necessarily extremely) strong right arm. Compressed air and vacuum brakes were still non-existent: the driver could start a train, but he had to rely on others to stop it at all quickly, and sometimes at all.

CHAPTER NINE

Signals, Telegraphs and Train Working

Not only were trains faster than any other means of transport known before; they were slow to bring to a stop and could take no action to evade obstruction in their path. It was therefore realized from the start that careful precautions would be needed to ensure their safety. As G. D. Dempsey wrote in *The Practical Railway Engineer* in 1855:

> Without a system of well-arranged, well-understood, and faithfully-worked signals, it would be utterly impossible to conduct the traffic of any railway with safety and regularity. The 'all right' and 'hold hard' of the stagecoach, the 'go on', 'ease her', 'stop her', and 'half-turn astern' of the steamboat, are sufficient for the proper progress of those conveyances; but against the puff, whirr, the chatter of the *Vulcan*, the *Rocket*, the *Ajax*, the *Thunderer*, or the *Hurricane*, what human voice, even if pitched in the key of a Stentor, could possibly prevail?

However, there are several kinds of information that signals have to convey to the driver of a train. First of all, there is the question whether the line ahead is clear, or whether there is another train on it. Secondly, there is another question when approaching stations and junctions; are the points set for a diverging route for which speed must be reduced? Thirdly, and especially at night and in thick weather, it is important to give advance warning of any need to stop or slow down at a following signal that cannot yet be seen, so that the driver may start to pull up. Finally, there is also the question of how the guard (or passengers) may attract the driver's attention to the need to stop because of some misadventure on the train.

As far as the maintenance of an interval between trains proceeding in the same direction was concerned, this was originally the responsibility of specially appointed railway policemen, who had the duty of keeping a check on passing trains and giving a hand signal to the driver, either to slow down or to stop, or else to carry on unchecked, according to the time elapsed since a previous train had passed. In general, an interval of ten minutes was imposed, varying somewhat according to circumstances. The policeman was given many other responsibilities as well; to keep an eye on porters and others loading wagons, to prevent pilferage; to apprehend trespassers; to draw the attention of officers to anything unusual; and other various matters. It was not surprising that his hand signals were soon found to be inadequate, if only because drivers never could be sure where to look for him, so his tasks were divided. The railway police continued to exist, but a separate staff of men concerned only with train control was set up, and given the responsibility of operating a series of fixed signals, which began to be installed in the mid-1830s.

Quite a lot of experimentation went on to determine what kind of signal to use; the first on the Liverpool & Manchester, in 1834, was a simple lantern hung on the top of a post by night, showing either a red or a white light (for danger or clear). By day hand signals continued, and in order to change the colour displayed somebody had to climb a ladder and adjust the lantern. In 1838 Sir John Hawkshaw invented the disc signal, a flat plate at the top of a pole capable of being turned through 90° so that it either presented its full face or its invisible edge to a driver, with a lantern with two coloured lenses similarly attached for night use. This signal gave two readily visible aspects by night but only one by day, and was not very widely used in its original form. On the L & M in 1841 signals were displayed by a flag, either hoisted or not hoisted up a flagpole at each station; which was all very well so long as the wind was blowing, but not easy to read on a calm day. Other lines used systems of coloured boards placed on stands. There was at any rate some uniformity about the colours. White meant 'all clear', green 'caution', and red 'danger'. A white light at night was less confusing then than it would be now, with few if any street lamps and most houses lit only by candlelight; however, there must have been some confusion, since it is also recorded that a candle placed in the window of a local station near Stockton indicated 'stop, there is a passenger wanting to get on'. Again, when the York & North Midland opened its line from York to Whitwood Junction (Normanton), connecting with the North Midland from Derby (and thence London), in 1840, the signalling at Whitwood was rudimentary, consisting merely of a single board to discourage one or other of two simultaneously converging trains by day and a coal brazier by the lineside at night to give the driver warning of where he was and what the hazards were.

Even in the early days, the policeman had assistance from pointsmen at large stations; the task of these men was to set each point individually by hand as instructed. Inevitably there was some danger of misunderstandings as a result of this division of responsibility. To quote F. S. Williams, in *Our Iron Road* (1883):

> A station-master, or porter, might put signals at safety or danger, while someone else worked the points. Or it might be that the pointsman ran from his point to the signal lever, or back again. Or it might be, and too often it was the case, that the signals were not properly worked at all; the pointsman, perhaps, was fully occupied in pulling the one lever, and could not get at the other; or the signalman might vainly trust to the pointsman doing his duty and give the signal of safety when danger was imminent. Points and signals might thus be, and too often were, in direct contradiction, and the driver, relying on the safety which the lowered arm or the white light falsely bespoke, rushed confidently on his headlong way, to wake—if he ever woke at all—amid the crash of shattered carriages and the shrieks and groans of the wounded and the dying.

Thus a penny-a-line journalist's account of the matter, but there was something in what he said, and more in the sheer convenience of centralized working.

Hawkshaw's disc signal, modified by having a bar added at right-angles to the disc so that some aspect was always visible, was considerably used by the late 1840s, especially on the Great Western. When the disc was presented full-face to the driver, it signified 'clear'; the bar similarly meant 'stop'. Some use was made of 'fan-tail' signals, in which a cloth flag or blind was drawn out across a frame; these could be of several kinds, perhaps displaying two different colours; these were visible enough but proved very liable to damage from the wind and were abandoned after a few years.

A system of semaphore signalling had long been used by the Admiralty; a chain of hilltop relay stations between London and

Portsmouth and the Medway ports existed, and messages were passed in the same manner as that by which a man giving flag handsignals transmits a message from one ship to another. The first railway semaphores seem to have been used in 1839, at Corbets Lane, where the London & Croydon Railway joined the London & Greenwich, and to have been the responsibility of Hutton Gregory. These soon became much the commonest form of signal. In the shape standard from the mid-1840s until the 1870s, a railway semaphore consisted of one or more wooden arms hinged at one end and hanging in a slot at the top of the signal post. Three aspects were shown, based on the three standard hand signals given by the policeman; arm horizontal (stop); arm inclined downwards at 45° (caution); arm vertical, and concealed in the slot in the post, equivalent to the 'no-hand' signal given by the policeman standing to attention (clear). Very often the same post held signal arms for each direction; the driver could distinguish the one applying to him since it always protruded from the lefthand side of the post. There might be more than one arm for one direction, since in certain cases approaching junctions the 'clear' for a diverging route was given by the lower arm (a system which remains standard practice on many overseas railways), but normally in British practice a separate post was provided for the second route, as shown in plate 32. The signal post also carried a lantern, which either turned through 90° to display coloured lenses (white, green, red) or were fitted with moving spectacles with coloured glasses, in conformity with the position of the semaphore arms.

Both the disc-and-crossbar and the slotted-post semaphore were tolerably sound signals and remained in service on a large scale into the 1880s. Many railways used both, the semaphore as a positive instruction, and a disc signal as an 'auxiliary' or distant warning of the semaphore's aspect. However, with the increasing speed of trains, distant signals came to be needed almost universally, which had the effect of making a semaphore capable of giving three aspects redundant. The slotted-post semaphore was thus given its quietus after the Abbotts Ripton accident on the Great Northern in 1876, when an arm was frozen into its slot during a blizzard and gave a false 'clear' indication.

On the earliest lines there were few junctions, and it was possible to depend on handsignals or individually worked fixed signals to control them, particularly in combination with severe speed restrictions. In fact, working of this kind at junctions in mid-country, away from stations, lasted for a surprisingly long time. Nevertheless, there was a source of danger in the possibility that signals might indicate one thing, but points perform another; to obviate this it became necessary at long last to bring the levers controlling all the signals and points for the whole of each layout to one place, where they could be placed in one frame and interlocked mechanically in such a way that each had to correspond with all the others, while conflicting movements were made impossible. The actual locking method was basically simple, involving the use of a locking-bar moved by the rod attached to each lever, and catching or releasing rods attached to other levers; the complexity of a mechanical locking frame is simply due to the large number of permutations of movements that must be catered for, and hence the frame itself was a fairly expensive piece of apparatus that needed to be kept well maintained and under cover. Thus the signalbox, into which of course the signalman also moved, turning his well-lit upper floor above the machinery into a highly polished comfortably heated home away from home. (Not that earlier signalmen had remained particularly uncomfortable for long; a mere sentrybox was all that was provided in some places, but plate 33 shows a charming little early-day signalman's hut, with ivy on the walls and flowers in a windowbox, and nothing more to do than look after a pair of disc signals and a brace of hour glasses.)

But these improvements really lie beyond the date of this book. The first junction with any interlocking at all, and that only between signals, not between signals and points, was that installed at Bricklayer's Arms on the London & Croydon, again by Hutton Gregory, about 1840. It was not until 1856 that any attempt was made to interlock signals with points; this was by J. Saxby, on the same site, and was only partial. The first fully interlocked junction, with all possible conflictions barred, was not provided until 1860, and then only at the relatively modest pair of double-line junctions at Kentish Town (now Camden Road) on the North London line. It was a long time from then before the 100 per cent interlocking of all points and signals on every passenger line in the country, ordained by the Regulation of Railways Act 1889, was completed.

So during the period before 1860 effectively the only safeguard from collisions due to conflicting movements at junctions, or accidents due to trains being diverted on to the wrong line at speed, in cases where there was no driver error, was the reliability of the signalman. However, then as subsequently, they were in general a very competent body of men, recruited for good money at a time when the railways could afford to pick and choose their servants. In fact their mistakes were relatively rare; disasters at this period tended to show up shortcomings in the system or equipment more often than failures of the human element, bearing in mind that the system should itself contain safeguards against error.

The maintenance of an interval between trains moving in the same direction on the same line was the most important problem in the early days. The Stockton & Darlington was a single line at first, worked on fairly free-and-easy principles with passing loops at short intervals, a halfway post between every pair of them, and he who was first past the post was entitled to require anybody he met to retreat before him into a siding. Similarly, horse-drawn loads caught up from behind by steam engines had to pull to one side as soon as possible to let the monster past. But the Liverpool & Manchester, and most subsequent early lines, were double-tracked from the start. Trains going the other way were thus no problem (unless you were running late for some reason and they had sent an engine out along the wrong line to look for you and tow you home if necessary—a fairly frequent hazard in the early years, though the nimble-witted pilot drivers managed to avoid catastrophe surprisingly often). The method used on the L & M to keep trains apart was, by 1841, to display a red board for five minutes after a train had passed, followed by a green board for a further five minutes (unless the train was an express, or a special, when five minutes of green only sufficed). Similar methods were used on other lines. Since few railwaymen had watches, the policemen or signalmen were issued with sand-glasses.

The shortcoming of the time interval system was, of course, that it was a time and not a space interval. The obedient and industrious signalman, carefully following the rules, could confidently despatch train after train at top speed at eleven-minute intervals until some panting rustic informed him that the smoke rising behind yonder hill came, not from a bonfire but from a blazing heap of wreckage on which train after train was immolating itself, one every eleven minutes. Yet, short of smoke signals (on a rather less dramatic principle), there was no better way of doing things at first because there was no way of knowing whether train A was safely out of the way having passed some point further down the line, or whether it was halted broken down just round the corner.

The answer to the situation was the electric telegraph; yet it was adopted only slowly. The first telegraph installation in Britain was on the GWR between Paddington and Hanwell, opened by Cooke and Wheatstone in December 1839. There were several telegraph stations along the line, and the arrival, passing, or departure of each train was telegraphed between them, and instructions given that a second train should not be allowed to leave until the arrival of the first at the following station had been duly communicated. At first these messages were transmitted in plain language (or rather, in telegraphese), since the instruments were fitted with five or six needles in such a way that the convergence of any two of them would point out a letter of the alphabet on a grid, and the primary intention of the builders was to transmit general messages for the public. About seventeen words per minute could be sent. But it was in this way that the block system originated, and the value to the railway of this method of working was so apparent that in 1841 Cooke and Wheatstone produced a simplified two-needle telegraph instrument which transmitted three indications for each line: 'Stop' (needle inclined one way), 'Go on' (needle inclined the other way), and 'Neutral' (needle vertical). This gave all the information needed to work the block system, though in fact the meaning usually adopted was not quite as simple as that, but rather 'line clear' and 'train on line'. The first really successful specialized railway telegraph was different again, being devised in 1840 to meet the rather special working needs of the cable-operated London & Blackwall railway, where in the up direction a carriage set off simultaneously from every station, arriving successively at the Minories terminus, and it was therefore necessary for each station to signal to the engineman that all was clear to start winding.

The idea of the block system was strongly opposed by many railway companies, probably on the grounds of expense, though as one contemporary writer had it 'the fundamental principle of the "block" was at first derided, and the name chosen was considered as characteristic of the condition traffic was likely to get into under any such system of working'. Nevertheless, common sense and the sustained pressure of the Board of Trade brought about a slow but steady increase in the length of railway telegraphs. In 1841 the London, Brighton & South Coast installed block working in the Clayton Tunnel; in 1845 the Bristol & Gloucester in Wickwar tunnel; in 1846 the Midland in Thackley, Cleugh and Duffield tunnels, and in 1848 throughout the heavily tunnelled length between Ambergate and Rowsley. In 1851 the South Eastern completed the installation of the telegraph and block working all the way between London and Dover, and in 1853 the London & North Western, having already installed it between London and Carlisle, began to apply it throughout their main lines. It is significant to notice the choice of some of these routes for the first continuous telegraphs, for they were not intended solely for railway use. Several wires were reserved for the transmission of public messages, and in the Railways Clauses Consolidation Act of 1846 the government took powers to compel the railways to provide facilities for this purpose. In fact, the spread of the telegraph was a joint enterprise of the various railways and the Electric Telegraph Company, which had succeeded in demonstrating that by providing a public service in this way the business could be run at a profit. So it could, and once this was realized the telegraph at last spread like lightning; by 1856 no less than 7200 miles of railway were equipped. One might remark at this point that during the early 1870s the Electric Telegraph Company was acquired by the government, and thereafter its profitability declined; but this is by the way. The actual wires and equipment along the railways remained railway property.

Edwin Clark's apparatus, used by the London & North Western, is a good example of the normal pattern of block telegraph used during the 1850s. Unlike the modern block instrument, which is normally at rest with no current passing, a current flowed continuously through the Clark instrument, whose normal indication, with the needle inclined one way, was 'line clear'. As a train passed one box, the signalman reversed the direction of the current, and the needle swung the other way to read 'train on line'; it could not be restored to its first position except by the signalman at the next box, as the train passed him. The telegraph wire was carried in a loop halfway down every post along the line, and the train crews were instructed in case of breakdown or accident to cut it; thus a vertical needle was intended as an emergency, or 'line blocked' indication.

In principle this was a good idea, but in practice it gave rise to too many false alarms, so the principle of cutting the wire was after some years abandoned. Originally the wires themselves were of galvanized iron, one-tenth of an inch in diameter; but by 1855 copper was universal because of its better conductivity and freedom from corrosion.

Apart from the block telegraph, the railway company soon found it useful to maintain its own private lines to pass administrative messages. There was a considerable saving to be made, for instance, by telegraphing instructions for the despatch of empty wagons so that they were sent to stations which needed them; in this way it was no longer necessary to maintain at each station a stock of empties large enough to cater for every possible flow of traffic. Other ways in which the telegraph eased working similarly will come to mind. Mark Huish, of the L & NW, wrote of the vast number of extra trains run to cater for the crowds attending the Great Exhibition of 1851:

> From the very great distance many of these trains had to travel before reaching the North Western, dependent in many cases also on steamboats and the delays incident on overcrowded trains, it was impossible to rely on any timebill, while the number of these excursion trains, amounting sometimes to twenty or thirty a day, many of them not known to be en route until they reached one or other terminus of the line, also meant that without the telegraph the traffic could not have been passed [since arrangements could not have been made for it].

The Morse Code was not universally used by any means on these telegraphs, but various private codes were used instead. Some of the codes provided read oddly now; the Stockton & Darlington's telegraph through Shildon Tunnel in 1860 included one meaning 'I am showing the telegraph to a friend'.

There were some odd sorts of telegraph machine: one, patented by Nott in 1846, involved the electrical control of the pallet of a ratchet, causing a clockwork-powered wheel or needle to rotate to a certain point, corresponding to a given message or code. A few examples of this apparatus, used as train describers, survived into the 1950s, including a fine example at Shrewsbury.

The telegraph was also used to control traffic on single lines. In theory, of course, it is as reliable a method of working there as on double track; if the block telegraph can prevent two trains from occupying the same length of rails at the same time, it does not matter whether they are both wishing to proceed in the same or in opposite directions. This commonsense view was adopted at first, and the single line of the Norfolk Railway between Norwich and Yarmouth was one of the first continuous lengths in the country to be equipped with a throughout telegraph, in 1848. Others followed, and it became the standard method of working busy single tracks. But there was always the danger of a false message, a misunderstanding of some kind, and the consequence of this on a single line would be much more likely to cause a disaster. Oddly enough, it was on the pioneer length near Norwich, a matter of days before the line was doubled, that the accident occurred which first discredited this system of working in Britain; a head-on collision of two pasenger trains on 10 September 1874 brought about by the responsible official first deciding to alter the timetabled crossing point of the two trains because one was running late and telegraphing ahead to bring on the other train, and then forgetting he had done so and despatching the first. This occurred on a well run railway; but on 7 August 1876 another head-on collision took place at Radstock, on the Somerset & Dorset, a line of quite another kind, which used a similar telegraph system. These two accidents emphasized that the single line telegraph gave no safeguard in the case of human error, and that something more positive was needed.

This was provided by a reversion in principle to earlier practice. On the rare single lines during the 1840s which were not short branches worked by one engine at a time, it was customary for every section to have a pilotman, who either rode on, or (if two trains were due to follow one another) gave a ticket to the driver and thus despatched every train personally. This is still the ordinary method used when one track on a double line is temporarily out of action; about 1860 it was realized that it was not necessary to have an actual man, a piece of wood would do, and this was the origin of the 'staff-and-ticket' system. Each staff is clearly labelled with the length of line it covers, and a driver may not enter that length unless either he carries the staff, of has been shown it and given a written instruction to proceed. The further modification of this system, by which many identical tokens exist for each section, but are stored in electrically interlocked machines at each end of it that will only release one at a time, was due to Edward Tyer in 1878.

Interlocking and the various telegraphs and staff systems guarded against most types of signalman's error; but there was still one considerable loophole, in that there was no check against the driver who misread or disobeyed a signal indication. The difficulty was to find some means of either attracting his attention or somehow stopping the train without him. In 1852 Tyer devised an apparatus depending on ramps in the track connected with the signals and striking triggers on the engine, but no purely mechanical system could stand the strain of sharp blows and impacts on necessarily complex linkages at speed. No satisfactory device was produced during the nineteenth century for this purpose, and for the same reason no reliable means of working signals automatically was found, though as early as 1841 C. B. Curtis had patented and described an automatic signal controlled by a clockwork timer set off by the trigger on a passing engine. But automatic devices which are not absolutely reliable are worse than useless, and people remembered the part played by one which failed to return to danger in bringing about the accident in Clayton Tunnel, despite the electric block, on the London, Brighton & South Coast in 1861.

The other direction from which a driver's attention might have to be attracted was from the train, and here inventors had a freer run. By the 1850s a communication cord consisting of a line run on hangers outside each coach, which could be reached by putting an arm out of a window, and which in principle rang a gong on the tender, was the standard fitting. But it was not very satisfactory; there were problems about adding or taking off coaches; the line had to be kept fairly slack to allow for the stretch of the couplings, etc.; and one tended to have to draw in several armfuls before much (if anything) happened. It was rather more important that the guard should have a reliable means of communication, and several were proposed. Wickens patented, and demonstrated in 1855 on the L & SWR, a train pipe with a whistle attached, into which one could blow. His suggested code of whistle signals included 'Go Faster—Behind Time—Another Train Following'; one imagines the guard desperately panting into his mouthpiece as the hungry buffers of the express drew closer. In the same year, Captain Norton (RN) gave railway engineers the benefit of his advice on the subject, based on his study of ancient and oriental weaponry. He suggested the use of a whistling bolt, analogous to the whistling arrow used by the Chinese army, fired by the guard from a crossbow or a rifle and aimed a few yards over the driver's head, the latter being protected from possible accident by a stout shield or screen. Alternatively, a one-pound paper bag of gunpowder, with a slow-match attached, should be raised at the end of an eight-foot iron pole by the guard (who would presumably keep his eyes skinned for overbridges, etc.); its flash 'would resemble lightning, or the blowing up of an ammunition wagon', and attract attention. Alternatively again, such a bag could be hurled fifty feet in the air by a catapult or ballista in the guard's van; presumably the intention was that it should explode at that height, rather than in the van or on impact. There is no record that any railway company allowed the gallant Captain to test any of his inventions on their line; one feels that if they had, there would have been. The problem of passenger communication is another one that was not satisfactorily solved until near the turn of the century, with the fitting of universal continuous brakes.

Behind all the slowly increasing mechanical complexity of devices intended to maintain safety, stood the men who had the responsibility of working the trains, and upon whom in the last resort everything depended. Many of the early accident reports make rather jolly local-gossip type reading. Thus Ritchie:

> On January 13th [1846] a somewhat alarming collision took place on the Cleland Railway, close to its junction with the Wishaw & Coltness line, at the Holytown station. The wooden waggon which leaves the Newarthill depot at 9 a.m., with passengers for the Wishaw & Coltness train to Glasgow, was proceeding rapidly in this manner towards its destination, when whether from neglect on the part of its conductor, or the insufficiency of the drag, we know not, it came into violent contact with some stationary trucks at Holytown station: and the passengers' waggon being unprovided with buffers, springs, or anything that could soften the effect of such a collision, the whole of the passengers were projected roughly forward.

To which, tut-tut seems about the strongest sort of comment that can be offered. And yet, though many of the mishaps had their comic aspect, the damage and suffering that resulted from the more serious ones was considerable. Even the opening day of the Liverpool & Manchester was quite bad enough really, leaving aside the complication of a near-riot which developed.

An interesting account of some of the kinds of mischance that occurred is given in a book misleadingly entitled *Railway Locomotive Management*, by 'Veritas Vincit', published in 1847. The author was probably John Robertson, a journalist on the staff of the *Railway Times*, who took the part of the enginemen of the North Midland Railway during a dispute with the management in 1842–3. The cause of the dispute was the company's wish to alter the conditions of employment; originally these were that drivers were paid 7*s* per day and firemen 4*s* per day, seven days a week. For two weeks out of three the men ran trains for three days then had one 'shed' day, either resting or repairing their engine; for the third week they were on pilot duty, working as required. The proposal was that firemen's pay be cut to 3*s* 9*d*, and that only six days a week be paid, the seventh being a day off. The book, a collection of letters to the editor, is good reading in a tedious sort of way, pretty scurrilous and onesided; the author was a terrible trade unionist. He had a nice turn of phrase: 'it is also an undeniable fact that, among the petty locomotive superintendents [i.e. shed foremen] who are as common as locusts and as vain and intelligent as peacocks, nine-tenths of them could not tell what was the matter with an engine unless the engineman informed him'; or, having a dig at Matthew Kirtley's draughtsman—'Master Haydon, more famous for the outside garniture of his head than for its furniture within'. But some of his antagonists were not too bad either; one described the author as 'a man whose mechanical knowledge barely enables him to distinguish between a locomotive and a wheelbarrow', which seems a just comment on the complaint quoted above regarding shed foremen, who can hardly be expected to be able to know what is wrong with a locomotive on the road from just looking at it standing still. Some account is given of a number of accidents, most of them trivial but one fairly nasty collision. But the general standard of argument is illustrated by a diatribe on unpunctuality. 'During the last four weeks the delays have amounted to 3,468 minutes. As one fatal accident was occasioned by a delay of 12 minutes, it is just a simple question of the Rule of Three, that 289 such collisions would be liable to take place in 3,468 minutes.'

A little more informative was a paper delivered by Mark Huish before the Institution of Civil Engineers in April 1852, covering accident experience and safety measures on the London & North Western over four years. Accidents due to defective track were rare, but vandalism was worrying. Facing points had been kept down to the smallest possible number, since in those days they were not interlocked and still locally controlled; self-acting or sprung switches were not reliable. Wheel failures on passenger coaches were (said Huish) fairly rare, with only six in four years, but hot boxes were frequent. There had been no serious case of fire in a passenger train, but some incidents had been potentially serious and the carriage of inflammable goods by freight train was often positively dangerous, since the railway had quite inadequate powers to control the necessary safeguards, especially on private owners' wagons. (The appalling fire following the collision at Abergele between the Irish Mail and some runaway wagons containing oil underlined the prophetic nature of Huish's words here, but this happened fifteen years later in 1867 and nothing had improved meanwhile.) No satisfactory communication system for passengers had yet been devised; the L & NW did the best it could by putting the guard in a lookout window protruding a foot beyond the side of the train, with instructions to keep a sharp lookout.

Freight stock was not apparently in a very satisfactory state: wheels and axles were markedly more prone to failure than on passenger stock, and an improvement in their quality at any rate to passenger standards was essential. Buffers and couplings were also poor, and few wagons yet had spring buffers; moreover, there was a great lack of uniformity in buffer height between wagons belonging to different companies and in different states of loading and repair, and this was also dangerous. As to other causes of accidents, falling trees by the lineside were significant and cattle on the line and at level crossings were a menace. As to safeguards, Huish spoke of the recent introduction of 'lofty semaphores' visible for 800–1500 yards, and of the also new system of using detonators as fog signals.

An analysis of causes of 1000 locomotive failures on trains was also given in the paper. Much the most frequent cause of trouble was breakage of parts of moving machinery—49 per cent; 16 per cent of failures were due to burst or leaky tubes, 10 per cent to broken springs, 8 per cent to broken pipes connected to the feedpump

(failures of the feedpump itself and its driving rods and links being included with valve gear failures); broken wheels, axles, and tyres 4 per cent (but of course with generally far worse results than any of the preceding causes); broken firebars 3 per cent, boiler defects 2 per cent, and then a long string of miscellaneous troubles, including 'smokebox on fire (3)' and 'boiler explosion (1)'. Not in fact a remarkably different proportion of causes to that in the last years of steam, though wheels, axles, tyres, and boilers were no longer significantly dangerous and the abolition of the feedpump clearly got rid of a very present cause of trouble.

Huish ended with a tribute to the men who ran the trains, on whom so much in the last analysis depended.

> There is probably no class of men, to whom such serious duties are entrusted, and who repay with such fidelity, attention, and skill, the confidence reposed in them. Kind and considerate treatment, and good wages, combined with the utmost strictness of discipline, a readiness to reward merit, and a rigid determination to punish severely every dereliction of duty, are the best means of forming good and attentive servants. . . . Experience very clearly shows that in general better results have been obtained by rewarding obedience than by the greatest severity in punishing misconduct.

The last two sentences seem to modern readers to contain a contradiction; but in fact they did not. The point of severe punishment was not victimization; it was to weed out those who were not fitted to bear their responsibility. Where so much depended on men being able to trust each other to follow a fixed routine precisely, there was no room for the undependable, and his fellow workers would not wish to continue alongside him. It was not a harsh code really; it was a very fair one.

CHAPTER TEN

The Railway Age, 1860-1960

Perhaps the fact that this book is one of a series dealing with industrial archaeology gives the best excuse for its terminating an account of railway mechanical development around 1860. But there are other reasons. One is the fact that during the 1860s steel began to replace wrought iron; a result of this was that machinery made of steel was on the whole longer lasting, and although equipment (including even some locomotives and rolling stock) built during the 1860s and 1870s survived in service here and there into quite recent times, not much that was in use during the 1850s lasted into the twentieth century. Another reason was that after the 1860s, as there had been after 1835, there was a slowing up of new invention, and a pause (this time lasting into the 1880s) for consolidation.

Some of the most important subsequent developments have been mentioned already. For instance, the growth in comfort, spaciousness, and therefore weight of passenger coaches from about 1880. This led to an increase in locomotive size and power, bringing about in turn improvements in brakes, since earlier hand-worked methods could no longer deal with the heavier and faster trains. In turn, especially after the turn of the century, the use of steel for carriage building—first frames, then bodies—greatly increased train weights again, and set the cycle off once more. It was not until the 1930s that serious efforts began to be made to get the tare-weight per passenger figure to start to come down again, and not very much progress has been made since (arguably some of it has been due to a recent decline in standards of comfort). The interaction between train weight and engine size is well enough described by many, and there is no need to go over the process in detail. There is just one aspect of the matter which deserves attention here, and that is the question of freight wagons.

Britain's railways were unique in that, like no others in the world, the largest and most powerful locomotives in the mid-twentieth century were used for passenger traffic. It is an exaggeration to say that there had been no progress in freight locomotives since 1860; but there had been remarkably little. F. W. Webb on the London & North Western had introduced 0–8–0s and 2–8–0s for main line work after 1892; the 2–10–0 had to wait until 1943. For a century the 0–6–0 tender engine remained the typical British goods locomotive, while the passenger evolution ran from the 4–4–0 to the Atlantic, 4–6–0, and Pacific. There was progress in design, certainly; but not much in output. British freight trains throughout the whole period, with no very important exceptions, continued to consist of small four-wheeled wagons, with no continuous brakes (the provisions of the Regulation of Railways Act 1889 applied only to passenger trains), and still coupled together as they had been in the 1840s. The solitary real advance lay in the abolition of the wooden dumb buffer; apart from this, the only significant change in freight rolling stock was an increase in ordinary maximum capacity from about 6 to about 20 tons per wagon. Not remarkable for a hundred years. No wonder the motive power situation languished also. In Europe, where all freight stock was fitted with continuous brake but where buffers and couplings were unchanged, freight locomotives by 1900 were at least comparable in size with passenger; in America, where all freight stock was fitted with continuous brake and where the original link-and-pin couplings were replaced by the Janney automatic coupler in the 1880s, freight locomotives tended to be very considerably larger.

There are four ways in which locomotive design made progress over the period. Engines became larger and more powerful; they began to use superheated steam; the performance of their valves and cylinders was improved; and the design and layout of their mechanical parts became stronger and more practical. Enough has been said already about the first. The second was at least as important.

The trouble about using steam taken directly from the boiler to the cylinders is that it is 'saturated', on the very borderline between liquid and gas. It contains a certain amount of water in droplet form, and if it is cooled or expanded at all (as of course happens in the cylinder) condensation starts at once and more water is formed. Since this takes up less volume than steam the pressure is reduced more than proportionately to the expansion. In addition, this means that hot water gets passed through the cylinders; it does no work, but represents a considerable amount of waste heat, and therefore fuel. If the steam can be reheated, or 'superheated', not only is it dried completely, but if the degree of superheat is sufficient it remains free of condensation until it has passed to the exhaust. This saves fuel directly, and also indirectly, since it is then possible for the steam to be expanded more in the cylinders and thus obtain a greater amount of work from it. The development of a workable locomotive superheater was due to Wilhelm Schmidt of the Prussian State Railways about 1900, though there had been earlier experiments, including the use of steam drums in the smokebox which may have achieved a certain amount of steam drying when the engine was working really hard; among others, McConnell on the L & NWR in 1852 and Aspinall on the L & YR in 1899 used such devices.

The Schmidt superheater, which within fifteen years from its introduction to Britain in 1906 had become a standard fitting on practically all main line engines, consists of a number of U-shaped tubes or 'elements', held inside an equivalent number of boiler tubes of specially large diameter, or 'flues'. Steam from the boiler passes through the elements, and is heated by the hot gases moving through the flues; the degree of superheat obtainable depends on several factors, including the number of elements and how hard the engine is working (in each case the more the higher).

The greater capacity of superheated steam to expand began to cast light on deficiencies in cylinder performance in two ways. First there was the problem of lubrication; saturated steam was kind in this respect, since the water it contained was a reasonably good lubricant anyhow. But the use of hot, dry, steam soon caused the amount of wear and tear to rise, especially in the valves. The slide valve, which had given good service since Murray's time, could not deal with more than a very slight amount of superheat, because of the considerable friction resulting from the flat valve being pressed down onto the flat working surface. Various attempts had been made during the nineteenth century to use piston valves instead, which had much less friction because there was no force pushing the piston against the walls of the cylinder in which it worked; they failed, since there was difficulty in keeping the valve steamtight and insufficient reason to press for a solution. Smith, on the North-Eastern railway, developed a workable piston valve in 1887, but it was little used until, with superheating, the matter became urgent. Schmidt's broad-ring piston valve was widely adopted at first, but the modern narrow-ring valve, also of German origin, was introduced during the 1920s and thereafter became universal.

The more subtle effect of superheating on cylinder and valve design took longer to emerge; G. J. Churchward at Swindon was perhaps the first to appreciate it. Now that really short cut-offs, below 25 per cent, began to be practical, it was important to make sure that the steam could be got in and out of the cylinders freely and fast. The old Stephenson gear with short-travel valves could not do the job, since as we have seen lead became excessive at short cut-off and the steam was 'wire-drawn' through restricted port openings. Churchward therefore boldly altered the eccentric settings so that there was negative lead in full gear on all his two-cylinder engines and combined this with an increased length of travel, so obtaining Stephenson-gear engines that could run fast at short cut-off. Other designers, and Churchward himself when cramped for space in the four-cylinder *Star* class, opted instead for Walschaerts gear, which at last came into its own. The need for really large and unconstricted steam passages, which involved using large valves with long travel, meant a reversal of slide-valve practice, where in order to limit friction and the considerable amount of power needed to drive the valve it had been thought desirable to keep the travel short and the valve as small as practical. Finally, with the use of short cut-offs it was desirable to increase the lap of the valve; again, Churchward was the first twentieth-century designer to fully realize this, but the superiority of his methods was shown to the world during the comparative trials in 1925 between a GWR *Castle* 4–6–0 and a much larger, but at that time certainly no more effective, LNER *Gresley* 4–6–2. Gresley took the point well enough, and altered his engines accordingly; had the trial been repeated afterwards the result might have been different! There had been pioneers of long-lap, long-travel valves earlier, however, including Benjamin Connor of the Caledonian with his 8 ft 2 in 2–2–2s of 1862, which were notably good runners.

With superheating and improved cylinders and valves, it became possible at last to build locomotives capable of running at 100 mph. There are countless legends of locomotives reaching speeds of this order before 1920 in many countries, some of which are extremely unlikely; the brutal truth is that there is not one single fully credible or adequately proven case of the 100 mph mark being passed by any locomotive on any railway anywhere, including *City of Truro*, and all American apocrypha, until the trial runs of the 1930s, notably on the LNER. But by that time there was a commercial need for very high speeds, in order to meet the increasing competition of other means of transport; and in Britain, Germany, and the USA steam locomotives capable of doing the job were built at this time.

The final avenue of progress in steam locomotive design was in improving details to make their parts stronger, longer-lasting, or more accessible for repair. Fundamental to all this was the increasing need for economy in maintenance; after 1914 the time when the railways could command as much skilled and willing labour at as cheap a price as they wanted began to draw to a close. After 1945 the process gathered pace greatly, with the result that the series of BR standard locomotives which appeared during the 1950s was designed with accessibility and simplicity very much in mind, taking precedence for instance over any desire for ultimate economy in fuel consumption. It was in fact this strong pressure of economics that finally swept Britain's railways clear of steam power during the 1960s; a parallel transformation of the labour situation in the mining industry having sent up the price of coal beyond the point at which the steam locomotive could compete with its electric or diesel rivals, even if other things had been equal.

The motive power situation on today's railways, as compared with those of a century ago, has therefore been transformed; but only very recently. Till 1950 one could speak of evolution; the revolution is new. The rolling stock picture is similar, especially on the freight side, with vast changes in the last decade in the size and nature of vehicles. The traditional small four-wheeler still exists, but not, one feels, for much longer. On the passenger side, one may still talk of evolution at the moment, but some curious shapes of things to come are indicated.

The traditional fully interlocked mechanical signalling system, as we have seen, evolved fairly slowly and did not become universal until after the 1889 Act; it has been under challenge for thirty or forty years by the automatic colour-light, and is now very clearly on the way out, to be replaced by remote-controlled electrical installations, where trains over a considerable area, of the order of 100 route miles or more, are brought under the surveillance of men at one central point. Once again, the main reason for the change is economics, and the need to reduce manpower. (One should emphasize that 'economics' does not necessarily mean that there is a financial saving to the railway out of the changeover; very often, and in this case, there is not!) Perhaps the only type of railway which has changed in no very fundamental way over the last hundred years is the urban and suburban line, whether underground or surface; steam traction especially on the former had in general disappeared during the early years of the century, and automatic signalling came very early; but the purpose of this kind of railway remains unaltered, the carriage of passengers over relatively short distances, chiefly to and from work.

In fact, the most important differences between today's railway system and that of the 1860s are not really mechanical at all: the fundamental change is one of motive. During the nineteenth century, and effectively for the first half of the twentieth, railways existed purely and simply because they were the only practical means of inland transport. Not just 'the best': the 'only practical'. There had been roads with horses and carts; there had been canals. Neither of them could compete with the railway; therefore neither of them were practical. There were really only used where a railway was not available, or over very short distances to avoid transhipment. Thus there was tremendous pressure to build railways to serve every nook and cranny of the land, wherever any sort of case at all could be got up to prove that there would be sufficient traffic to make them pay. Many of the cases were pretty implausible even when the lines were built. The biggest financial disaster of all was unquestionably the Great Central's London Extension; several railways of considerable length, such as the Midland & Great Northern and the Somerset & Dorset, were always pretty hopeless financially but were rescued from their improvident promoters and licked into shape for the public benefit by large main line companies, who in turn built branches of their own with pretty poor prospects individually, but with the objective of serving the whole nation with a comprehensive network which paid its way overall.

Nowadays the situation is fundamentally different. The railway is not by any means the only practical means of inland transport. In several ways, the road haulier provides a better service for many types of freight; he can handle it without transhipment from door to door, and give it the driver's individual attention to guarantee its security *en route* and a dependable time of arrival. The railway can only provide the same standard of service in a few cases where articles move in trainload lots, and so in the long run it cannot hope to retain freight which does not fall into this category (except for some bulky, low-value traffic, like coal, where dependability of arrival is unimportant). On the passenger side, the bus has proved a cheaper and more flexible means of handling light flows over fairly short distances, while the private car, though expensive, is of quite matchless convenience and fully competitive for speed over increasing lengths of journey. (The introduction of car heaters as standard fittings in the 1950s will be seen by historians as a serious blow to the railways, since it signalled the end of any idea that the car was primarily for Summer or pleasure use.) Over longer distances, where the train still has the edge over the car for speed and convenience, the aeroplane competes increasingly strongly.

As a result of all these things the role of the modern railway has shrunk drastically. There is no longer any need for full geographical coverage, and by 1970 nearly 35 per cent of the original British railway route mileage had been abandoned (a higher proportion, perhaps, than in any other large country, with the possible exception of France, where the completion of remote rail feeders was in any case carried considerably further). The old legal 'common carrier' obligation, under which the railways were obliged to transport whatever articles were offered to them at a standard scale of charges, has been removed; they now need carry only what they want to carry. Road transport has taken over nearly all the work of local collection and delivery; trips by local freight train, delivering individual wagons to hosts of private sidings or small stations, have nearly ceased. Much hope is placed in containers, which can be loaded at point of origin, road hauled to a railhead, transhipped to a fast 'liner train' and whisked to another railhead, transhipped to road again, and hauled to destination; though in a country the size of Britain it surely seems unlikely that such complexity, and the maintenance of two fleets of road vehicles as well as a railway, can really be justified for the sake of a short trunk haul by rail. In fact, the only really cheerful picture on today's railways is presented by medium-distance intercity passenger traffic, and by concentrated bulk flows of special freight, neither of which will demand the maintenance of a large network of routes. Suburban passenger traffic hardly presents a cheerful picture, but it still remains one in which the railway performs an irreplaceable function.

The Railway Age is therefore over. Perhaps, in fact probably, railways in Britain will continue to have a useful part to play; but they will be physically very different from the railways of the past, and their function will be only a part of what it used to be. In their great days, the railways were, first and last, a public service, and the railwaymen consciously or unconsciously took pride and status in the community from this. Their jobs were relatively well paid, and highly responsible; in a very real sense the community depended on them. This was reflected by the degree of public interest in railway matters—very often perhaps critical and unfriendly interest, like some of Queen Victoria's fulminations to Gladstone on the excessive number of accidents, but also very often a close and friendly interest. There was a romance of the rail which sprang from the very fact that railways were vital; there was nothing nostalgic then about the public interest in them, it was based on pride in and admiration for current achievement.

Nowaday part of the situation is still the same; there is a genuine admiration for the progress made by the viable parts of the system, and the men who work on these lines still have a responsible and well-paid task. Even if the old absolute dependence of the community on them has largely gone, they can still take a well justified pride in their efforts; they are not wasting their time. But the current situation is bedevilled by the fact that much of the rest of the network remains, not because it is important or even much used by the community any more, but out of inertia. It is subsidized to keep it alive, and to keep the men in work. It has become a form of outdoor relief; those employed can have little pride in their tasks and even less hope for their future. There is, true, a considerable public interest in these lines, but it is fundamentally a nostalgic one, and sometimes not healthy nostalgia but a morbid and inward-looking variety. Anybody who has true respect for railway history and achievement, and a proper understanding of what railways can still do for the community, can only hope devoutly that all the remaining lines of this kind are exterminated as soon as possible.

It may yet be that in the history books of the future the story of railways will be told in terms of the story of the steam age: that 120 years of steam haulage will outweigh *N* more recent years of other traction. Certainly it is the steam locomotive that has already passed into folklore, and has a hold on the public imagination that its rivals have never approached. Countless American (and now European) infants are puzzled by their parents crying out 'Look, there's a choo-choo' as a diesel rumbles past. Certainly the efforts made here and there to preserve operating steam railways arouse a considerable and welcome amount of public interest and support. But against a great deal of the evidence one still hopes that the technical possibilities offered by the steel wheel on the steel rail, running along a private right-of-way, will still prove saleable. It is road transport that is threatening to pollute and strangle our cities, and to make an uproar of the countryside, and railways could still do much to reduce this degradation. Ruskin fulminated against the desecration caused by a railway (now abandoned) through Monsal Dale: what would he have said about a motorway? But, the contradiction remains; if people have shown by their choice that they prefer to use the road, how in any free society can one reverse this?

The Victorians put much faith in the *deus ex machina*: a problem existed, nothing could be done about it, but surely somebody would invent or discover the answer. Well, they could and they did; but we don't much like some of the answers nowadays. No doubt the transport contradiction will get answered in the same way, let us hope more to our satisfaction. For transport is an important question. Transport is a form of communication; and a community lives only because there is communication between the people who compose it.

Bibliographical Notes

The amount of literature published on railways, as one might expect, was very large between the 1820s and 1850s. Authors were at first propagandizing for, and then describing, something quite new; and popular interest was kept up by the spread of new lines over the county together with the pace of technical improvement. From the 1860s the quantity of matter declined markedly, and consisted of technical and educational works, concerned to describe the innovations that continued (at a slower pace) and to train new generations of railway men; together with works dealing with the administration of railways, and their finance and politics. Historical and biographical writing was fairly rare during the nineteenth century, though there were some important books of this kind; the first beginning of the present great flood of historical, descriptive, evocative writing did not appear until the 1880s and 1890s (when perhaps the imminent extinction of Brunel's broad gauge gave an initial impetus), although a few volumes of personal, more or less anecdotal, material were published earlier.

The present author has no intention of producing even a select bibliography covering the field; it is too vast, and has been well charted *in extenso* by George Ottley in his monumental *Bibliography of British Railway History*. Instead, some notes follow on certain of the principal works consulted. A number of others have been sufficiently referred to in the text. Publication details are given in a consolidated list on page 167.

First and foremost of the contemporary technical descriptions of early railways comes Nicholas Wood's *Practical Treatise on Railroads*, of which the first edition was published in 1825; it sold well, and considerably revised and updated new editions were published in 1831 and 1838. It surveys the whole field in detail, especially concerning construction of track, locomotives, and rolling stock, with a great deal of data on research into friction, and on the practical performance of the various forms of mechanical and animal power on road, rail, and water. Subsequently some perhaps less well digested comparative statistics of financial results, based on early Liverpool & Manchester performance, were added. Wood's object was to lay the facts before a public which knew nothing of them, and this he does seriously and sensibly, and at some length. In 1846 R. Ritchie produced *Railways, their Rise, Progress, and Construction*, which was brought out by the same publishers and was in effect a fourth edition of Wood's book, condensing most of his original material and adding, perhaps less ably, some more recent information of a descriptive kind, including some reportage of accidents.

Following Wood, who used a number of drawings and whose book also contained some folding engraved plates, came several extremely large volumes mainly concerned to publish detailed drawings of every possible part of a railway, from the design of pumps and axles to station architecture (and layout) and signal-levers, as a guide to those engineers who were building new lines. In this way information regarding different practices was circulated, and the best gained acceptance; it is a pity that as new construction slowed (and engineers began to feel they knew it all already) the printing of such books became uneconomic after the 1860s. However, such periodicals as *The Engineer* continued. In some of these books the text was minimal, and of less importance than the drawings; with Wood the balance had been quite the other way.

One example of this kind of book was S. C. Brees's *Railway Practice*, which appeared (in five volumes) between 1837 and 1847. It is mainly concerned with civil engineering, but has some useful information on rolling stock, including French and Austrian. It might be mentioned that the French published at least as many books of this kind on an even larger scale, including Perdonnet and Polonceau's *Nouveau portefeuille de l'ingenieur des chemins de fer* (1857). G. D. Dempsey's *The Practical Railway Engineer* (1855) is a finely produced book which carries on Nicholas Wood's aim considerably more successfully than Ritchie, and in which the text is restored to predominance. D. K. Clark's *Railway Machinery* (1855) and *Railway Locomotives* (1860) are worthy of mention, but the *magnum opus* of mid-nineteenth-century technical literature on locomotives is Zerah Colburn's *Locomotive Engineering and the Mechanism of*

Railways, completed in 1864 after Colburn's death by D. K. Clark. This is a very full and detailed accont of locomotive technology in the then state of the art; and Colburn, who was an American, had his feet on the ground in a practical Yankee way. For instance, at one place he makes the point that engineers were mistaken in spending such efforts in search of coal economy. If the *whole* cost of fuel were saved, it would mean only $\frac{2}{3}$% extra dividend to shareholders. Repairs cost more than fuel; mechanical improvement was therefore more important than thermal improvement, though despised by the 'dilettant'. Colburn's book became something of a standard work, and deserved to.

Three other contemporary works will be mentioned here, apart from those otherwise referred to in the text. The Liverpool & Manchester, when it opened and during its construction, was an object of intense public interest, and perhaps the first of all the popularizing railway books was Henry Booth's *The Liverpool and Manchester Railway*, published in 1830. Booth was not only the Treasurer of the Company, but as we have seen a man of some mechanical ability, with a recorded share in the development of the multiple-tube boiler and the screw coupling. More even than that, he was a competent writer, and in addition to a good account of the history of the project (for public consumption) enlivened his narrative with some quite evocative descriptive passages.

Dionysius Lardner has had a bad press since E. T. MacDermot, writing his two-volume *History of the Great Western Railway* (1927–31), savaged him on behalf of his ancient adversary, Brunel. Certainly his judgment lapsed on occasion; apart from the Box Tunnel incident, he once committed himself to the proposition that if a train ran on an undulating railway at a certain low speed on upgrades and a certain high speed on downgrades, its overall average speed would be the average of the uphill and downhill speeds, thus falling into a boobytrap avoidable by the averagely cautious schoolboy. But, as one of the first men to see the need, in an industrial society, for somebody to explain the mysteries of science to the general public, he had a considerable reputation in the 1830s and 1840s, and did a great deal of essential basic research into railway matters himself. He wrote a host of books; a typical sample might be his *Report on the Determination of the Mean Value of Railway Constants* (1842), prepared at the request of the British Association for the Advancement of Science, and as a result of experimentation with special trains on the Liverpool & Manchester, Grand Junction, and Great Western railways, among other trials. By force of experiment, carried very much further than Nicholas Wood had been able to at Killingwoth, Lardner determined the nature of frictional and air resistance, and produced data, including a log of a journey from Liverpool to Birmingham in vast detail, to show that the Stephensonian rule-of-thumb principles of construction, to keep grades and curves as slight as possible, was needlessly expensive. He proved that curves of under a mile radius, and gradients of up to 1 in 200, might be used without practical disadvantage, and Locke and others listened. On the way, he demolished by experiment a suggestion of Brunel's that air resistance might be significantly reduced by a form of streamlining with a train 'having a pointed front like a ship's prow', by trials on Madeley Bank in July 1839.

Perhaps the best general account of early railways in Britain is given by John Francis, in *History of the English Railway* (2 vols, 1851). This is a sound, non-technical account; Francis was a writer on commercial and financial topics. He rather enjoys himself on certain subjects, notably the depredations of the brutal and licentious navvies, and the vitiated sons and dishonoured daughters of the country folk that they left behind them, but on such matters as the Railway Mania and the rise and fall of George Hudson he is extremely sound. However, he does not deal with technical detail, though he does write well of certain engineers.

Turning finally to recent books, which approach the subject as history rather than as exposition or memory, the two most useful works on locomotive history and development are probably E. L. Ahrons, *The British Railway Steam Locomotive*, 1825–1925 (1927, 1961), and J. G. H. Warren, *A Century of Locomotive Building* (1923; 1970), which is a Centenary History of Robert Stephenson & Co. Ahrons's is a wideranging book, full of essential information, but very scrappy and ill-organized with many traces of its origin in a series of magazine articles, and with a poor index which might otherwise have helped. The author did not live to complete and revise the book. Warren covers a much narrower field (though one wide enough to miss little of importance, since the firm was in such an outstandingly predominant position in the early years) and therefore presents a clearer and better told story.

On other mechanical matters, there is much less. So far as carriage construction is concerned, Hamilton Ellis enters a one-horse race with his *Nineteenth Century Railway Carriages in the British Isles* (1949), but does his usual workmanlike job despite the lack of competition, within close limits of space. Otherwise, and on wagons, there seems to be nothing in book form, though back numbers of *Engineering* in particular are goldmines, waiting to be attacked. Charles Hadfield's *Atmospheric Railways* (1967) is a useful summary; much was published contemporaneously, including pamphlets by the Samudas, but after the bubble burst a silence fell. A. R. Bennett, better known for his books on steam engines, published a paper on 'Electric traction', read to the East of Scotland Engineering Association on 19 March 1889, whose date makes it early enough to be useful to the antiquarian.

As regards general engineering history, the field is considerably wider, though little of it specially refers to railways. L. T. C. Rolt's biographies of I. K. Brunel and the two Stephensons deserve a place in any list: but the seeker of detailed information will find a treasure-trove bristling with further references in the five volumes of the *Oxford History of Technology* dealing with every aspect of manufacture and industry, to which the author records his final acknowledgements.

Bibliography

ACWORTH, W. M. *The Railways of England*, 1889; reprinted Ian Allan, 1964.
AHRONS, E. L. *The British Steam Railway Locomotive* 1825–1925, Locomotive Publishing Co., 1927; reprinted Ian Allan, 1963.
ARCHER, M. *William Hedley*, 3rd edn, Darlington, 1885.
AYTON, R. *A Voyage Round Great Britain in the Year* 1813, London, 1814 (vol. 2 for account of lines near Whitehaven).
BING, F. G. *The Grand Surrey Iron Railway*, Croydon, 1931.
BOOTH, H. *The Liverpool and Manchester Railway*, Liverpool, 1830.
BREES, S. C. *Railway Practice*, 5 vols, London, 1837–47.
CASSERLEY, H. C. *Preserved Locomotives*, Ian Allan, 1969.
CLARK, D. K. *Railway Locomotives*, London, 1860.
CLARK, D. K. *Railway Machinery*, London, 1855.
CLARK, D. K., and COLBURN, Z. *Locomotive Engineering and the Mechanism of Railways*, London, 1864.
CLARK, D. K., and DEMPSEY, G. D. *Rudimentary Treatise on the Locomotive Engine*, London, 1879.
CLEGG, and SAMUDA, *The Atmospheric Railway*, London, 1840.
CURR, J. *The Coal Viewer's Practical Companion*, London, 1797.
ELLIS, C. H. *Nineteenth-Century Railway Carriages in Great Britain*, Modern Transport Publishing Co., 1949.
FRANCIS, J. *A History of the English Railway*, London, 1851.
GALE W. V. K. *Iron and Steel*, Longmans, 1969.
GRAY, T. *Observations on a General Iron Railway*, Nottingham, 1821.
GRAY, W. *Chorographia*, Newcastle, 1649 (reprinted 1818, 1881).
HADFIELD, C. *The Atmospheric Railway*, David & Charles, 1967.
HEAD, SIR GEORGE. *Home Tour*, London, 1835.
LARDNER, D. *Railway Economy*, London, 1850.
LARDNER, D. *Report on the Determination of Railway Constants*, London, 1842.

MACDERMOT, E. T. *History of the Great Western Railway*, 2 vols, 1927–31; rev. by C. R. Clinker, Ian Allan, 1964.
MARSHALL, C. F. DENDY. *British Railways Down to the Year* 1830, Oxford University Press, 1938.
MORGAN, BRYAN. *Railway Relics*, Ian Allan, 1970.
MORGAN, BRYAN. *Civil Engineering: Railways*, Longman, 1971.
OEYNHAUSEN, C. VON. *Report on Railways in England*, 1826/7, reprinted in *Transactions of the Newcomen Society*, vol. 29, 1958.
OTTLEY, G. *A Bibliography of British Railway History*, Allen & Unwin, 1966.
PEASE, A. E. *Diaries of Edward Pease*, Darlington, 1907.
Railway Enthusiasts Directory, biennial, David & Charles.
RITCHIE, R. *Railways: their Rise, Progress and Construction*, Longman, 1846.
ROLT, L. T. C. *Isambard Kingdom Brunel*, Longman, 1957.
ROLT, L. T. C. *George and Robert Stephenson*, Longman, 1960.
ROLT, L. T. C. *The Mechanicals*, Heinemann, 1967.
SAMUDA, *see* Clegg, and Samuda.
'VERITAS VINCIT.' *Railway Locomotive Management*, Derby, 1847.
SINGER, C., ed. *A History of Technology*, 5 vols, Oxford University Press, 1954–58.
WARREN, J. G. H. *A Century of Locomotive Building*, Newcastle, Robert Stephenson & Hawthorn, 1923; David & Charles, 1970.
WOOD, N. *A Practical Treatise on Railroads*, Longman, 1825, 1831, 1838.
YOUNG, R. *Timothy Hackworth and the Locomotive*, London, 1923.

Places to Visit

As with books, so with railway relics; there are quite a lot about, and they are reasonably well referenced. So there is no pretence at comprehensiveness here; for a fuller list of what has been preserved and where, see for example Bryan Morgan's *Railway Relics* and H. C. Casserley's *Preserved Locomotives.*

The principal museums containing, or consisting of, interesting exhibits of railway equipment, can be divided into three classes; the national collections, publicly-owned provincial collections generally of local interest; and privately-owned provincial collections.

The first category contains only two museums, with perhaps two borderline cases. The Science Museum, South Kensington, London, has a relatively small but valuable railway gallery, mainly dating from the earliest years (some of the exhibits have been detailed in the text), but also including one major item of extraordinary modernity. The Museum of British Transport, at Clapham (also in London) while it remains, is also a large and fairly comprehensive collection, including road transport items, but mainly of later date than 1860. The bulk of the railway exhibits will, it is intended, be moved to York, where there is now one of the borderline cases; the old North Eastern company's Railway Museum, which naturally retains a predominantly local flavour at present but does have some items from other parts of the country. Perhaps the Royal Scottish Museum in Edinburgh is on the other side of the 'national' borderline, but it has some objects of more than local interest.

In the second category come museums at Glasgow, Birmingham, Leicester, and Swindon, which all contain some notable exhibits of local railway interest; the small one at Swindon, for instance, has a replica of one of the early (but conventional) GWR broad gauge locomotives. This is unusual, however, in the date it represents, since most of at any rate the larger relics are considerably more recent than 1860.

The third category, if it is confined to non-operating relics, consists primarily of only two establishments, both in Wales, the Narrow Gauge Railway Museum on the Talyllyn Railway at Towyn, with a small but interesting collection of items in its special field, and the Penrhyn Castle Museum near Bangor, which has a number of exhibits of local railway interest, including some worthy relics; the latest acquisition being a rare Crampton 0–4–0 from the 1840s which for ninety years had been immured remote from public view in an obscure corner of a slate quarry.

As the present author once wrote elsewhere, however, there is a world of difference between engines immobile in museums, all polished and glazed, and engines at work; one might liken it to the gap which yawns between the stuffed and mounted elephant and the great, irritable, beady-eyed, flatulent, and likeable beast that stands waving its trunk at you. Despite British Railways' present and surely unmaintainable refusal to allow its image to be tarnished by fumes other than diesel, it is possible as a matter of course to see steam engines in daily service on a number of railways during the summer season. Only two have locomotives and coaches dating from as far back as the 1860s; but all the original passenger stock and both original locomotives (1865) of the Talyllyn Railway are still in service, and several coaches and one locomotive of the Festiniog Railway (the latter now little used) date back to the same period. Both these lines are, of course, narrow-gauge.

This is not the place to give a comprehensive list of all the operating steam passenger-carrying railways in Britain, or of places open to the public where working locomotives may be seen; several convenient guides are published, including the biennial *Railway Enthusiasts' Directory* (David & Charles). None apart from the two mentioned really contain any large relics that date back over a century; their *raison d'être* is the preservation of an era much less distant, though now otherwise totally vanished, of steam transport on rail and indeed of local transport by rail. The principal operations of this kind, on which one may travel, are: the Bluebell Railway (Horsted Keynes to Sheffield Park, Sussex); the Dart Valley Railway (Totnes to Buckfastleigh, Devon); the Keighley & Worth Valley Railway (Keighley to Haworth and Oxenhope, Yorkshire); and the

Severn Valley Railway (Bridgnorth, Shropshire); while other narrow-gauge lines operate in Wales at Aberystwyth, Llanfair Caereinion, and up Snowdon. Worthy of special mention is the Tramway Museum (the electric variety is referred to) at Crich, Derbyshire.

Index

Italicised entries refer to locomotive names; italicised figures (thus: *5*) refer to plates.

WORKING MEN'S COLLEGE
LIBRARY